The Games Of MUSIC

BY RALPH BURTON

A PROVEN SEQUENTIAL APPROACH TO **COUNTING** AND **SIGHT READING** — TO BE USED IN CONJUNCTION WITH YOUR PRESENT **BAND/ORCHESTRA METHOD**

The Games of MUSIC

(Rhythmic Development)

+

Characteristic Sounds

(Tonal Development)

TURNS YOUR PRESENT BAND/ORCHESTRA METHOD INTO...

- 80% SIGHT-READING
- A SOURCE FOR ADDITIONAL MUSICAL INFORMATION

Acknowledgments

I would like to thank my wife Suzanne, daughter Sarah, and son Jacob for their support and understanding; my parents and grandparents for instilling in me the value of discipline in life; my teachers and colleagues who provided guidance, comments, and encouragement throughout the writing of this method; Don Braddy for his talents in computers and graphic designing; Mark Rogers, Director of Publications, and everyone at Southern Music Company who contributed to the publication of this counting method.

A special thanks to Arturo Valdez III for his foresight, confidence and support that provided the opportunity to put my ideas and concepts into practice.

Preface

THE GAMES OF MUSIC is a counting/sight-reading method designed to accompany your present band/orchestra method book. Whereas band/orchestra method books encompass music education as a whole, **THE GAMES OF MUSIC** focuses on the development of counting/sight-reading skills.

The development of this method is a result of numerous discussions with leading music educators and my experiences as a student, clinician, performer, and educator. Even though I feel very fortunate to have been associated with prominent musicians and educators throughout my musical career, I still observed many musicians who had problems counting and/or sight-reading. I believe the majority of these problems exist because of the methodology of counting, not the ability of the educator or student.

A major difference between **THE GAMES OF MUSIC** and conventional counting methods is the scope and sequence. Without reinventing the wheel, the massive amount of information required to perform music is presented in a new innovative sequence. New information is supplied when needed, which is not the case with conventional methods. By introducing new information at specific times, confusion is greatly reduced and what use to be chronic annual problems are solved before they become a problem. This "defensive counting method" results in a significatively higher percentage of student comprehension and early development of the physical and mental aspects of counting.

I feel confident that those of you who supplement your present band/orchestra method with **THE GAMES OF MUSIC** will be as impressed with the results as those who have already incorporated this method into their music curriculum. Successful music educators at every level feel there is a void in our music education system when it comes to a structured counting method that enables every student to understand and enjoy musical notation. Granted, there have been outstanding musical organizations developed without this method, but the issue is whether another method can develop counting/sight-reading skills more efficiently and successfully, and this method can. **THE GAMES OF MUSIC** works....... you can count on it!

Best Wishes,

OVERVIEW

EVERY RHYTHM EVER WRITTEN CAN BE PLACED IN 1 OF 4 CATEGORIES !

- ***SUBDIVISION***
- ***COMBINATION***
- ***TIE***
- ***SYNCOPATION***

SUBDIVISIONS & COMBINATIONS

Rhythms from each of these 2 categories must be performed in **1 BEAT !**

TIES & SYNCOPATIONS

Rhythms from each of these 2 categories require **more than 1 BEAT !**

SUBDIVISIONS : **1 beat** divided into **equal** notes. The *Subdivision* of 1 is the **"note in disguise"**/time signature note. All other *Subdivisions* are equal divisions of the "note in disguise"/time signature note.

COMBINATIONS: **1 beat** combining **2** or more **different** *Subdivisions* within **1 beat.** Take the **down beat** from one *Subdivision* and combine it with the **up beat** from a different *Subdivision.*

TIES: Rhythms that last **longer than 1 beat.** To the "note in disguise", tie more "notes in disguise"/time signature notes, *Subdivisions,* or *Combinations.*

SYNCOPATIONS: Rhythms that are formed by **dividing** *Subdivisions* or *Combinations* with the **"note in disguise"**/time signature note.

DIRECTOR AND STUDENT APPROACH TO SUCCESSFUL COUNTING

- *KNOWLEDGE*
- *COORDINATION*
- *CONCENTRATION*

Directors and students realize that problems in counting/sight-reading are due to either a lack of knowledge, coordination, concentration, or a combination of the three.

HOW TO USE THE GAMES OF MUSIC

DIRECTORS MANUAL

Whether you begin with counting, tonal production, or a combination of the two, you will achieve immediate results with **THE GAMES OF MUSIC**. Each lesson is designed to adapt to various class times and schedules. If you do not finish a lesson, begin the next class with a quick review of prior information.

LESSONS 1-8 ARE TO BE TAUGHT IN ORDER. Lessons 1 through 6 are intended as daily lessons. Lessons 7 and 8 will require more time for internalization. Remaining rhythms are to be taught when needed. Simply locate the desired rhythm in the TABLE OF CONTENTS for the appropriate lesson. All basic rhythms in the TABLE OF CONTENTS are in 4/4 or 6/8 time. If a rhythm appears in your band or orchestra method book that you have not discussed, simply tell the students how the rhythm is performed and that you will explain it at a later time. Information located on the "chalk boards" should be written on the board for students to copy in their counting notebook beginning on page 44 of the **student text**. Prior to teaching a lesson, refer to the *Comments* section located at the end of each lesson.

Once the students have internalized note values, administer the *5 Minute Test* on page 43 until the student misses two or less. It is also recommended that all students pass this test at the beginning, middle, and end of each school year. Beginning on page 44 you will find a cumulative test. Instruct the students as to which numbers of the written test they are to complete. Although the tests are very benificial, some schedules do not allow enough time for testing; those students will also develop exceptional counting/sight-reading skills. Following the tests are note value charts that may be used as review and/or assessment.

Located on page 60 is a GAMES OF MUSIC REVIEW SHEET that is to be given to the students at the beginning of the following school year. The CONVERSION CHARTS on pages 63 and 64 are to be completed by those who use counting syllables that are not utilized in THE GAMES OF MUSIC.

As for students who were taught rhythms using conventional methods, explain how **current rhythms in 4/4 time** relate to the **number symbols** associated with *Subdivision*, *Combination*, *Tie* and *Syncopation*. Once they understand the basic concepts, one can relate the information to the other time signatures and rhythms. **Sign language is intended for beginning level students only.**

STUDENT TEXT

The "chalk boards" are visual reminders for each new rhythm. Once the rhythmic concept has been internalized, students are to fill in the white boxes with the correct counting syllables and/or notation. The NOTE VALUE CHARTS beginning on page 39 are also to be completed with the correct foot symbols, counting syllables, and notation. If a student forgets a rhythm, they can refer to the QUICK REFERENCE CHART located on the back cover.

Rhythmic exercises consist of number symbols and notation. These exercises are to be used for internalization and sight-reading. DO NOT REHEARSE. If the desired results are not performed within 2 attempts, assess the possibilities as to why and re-teach. Students are to perform **number symbols** by counting out loud, sizzling, and performing on their instrument. Directors ask the following for **notated** exercises: 1. "What game is it and what is the note in disguise"? 2. "How many subdivisions of 1's, how many subdivisions of 2's"? (ask for all current rhythms) 3. "Name the **rhythms** in order". 4. "Count the rhythms out loud". 5. "Perform the exercise on your instrument". Exercises may also be diagrammed.

Students are to transfer the information you write on the board to their COUNTING NOTEBOOK, page 44.

SIGN LANGUAGE

Foot tap only (1) (2) (3) (4) (2/4) (4/2) 2 (tie)

R.H. L.H.

FOOT/NOTE SYMBOLS

The lines found above notation represent the number of notes/rests found on the down beat and the up beat. THESE LINES DO NOT REPRESENT THE EXACT LENGTH OF SOUND/SILENCE OR WHERE THE SOUND AND SILENCE ACTUALLY BEGINS AND ENDS (style, ie. staccato and legato, should be discussed after the students have internalized the basic rhythmic concept).

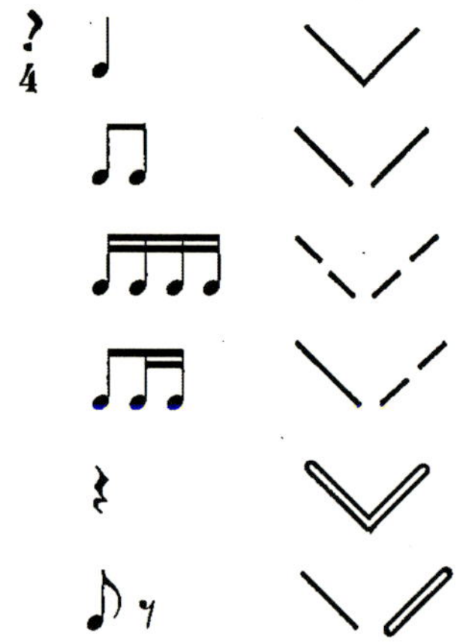

- One note lasting the entire beat.
- 2 notes, 1 beat. One note on the down beat and one note on the up beat.
- 4 notes, 1 beat. 2 notes on the down beat and 2 notes on the up beat.
- 3 notes, 1 beat. 1 note on the down beat and 2 notes on the up beat.
- The entire beat is silent.
- 1 note, 1 beat. 1 note on the down beat and a rest on the up beat.

NUMBER SYMBOLS

◯ - A circled number represents a *SUBDIVISION* rhythm.

(1) = Subdivision of 1/note in disguise (2) = Subdivision of 2 (4) = Subdivision of 4

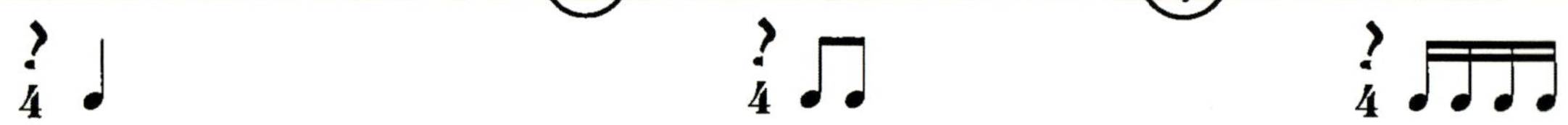

(/ - The letter "C" with a diagonal line represents a *COMBINATION* rhythm.

(2/4 = Combination 2 - 4 (4/2 = Combination 4 - 2

‿ - A number with a tie marking represents a TIE rhythm.

2 (tie) = Tie 2 4 (tie) = Tie 4

/ / - Two diagonal markings represents a *SYNCOPATED* rhythm.

2/1/2 = Syncopation 2-1-2 2/1/4 = Syncopation 2-1-4

Application of all visual techniques.

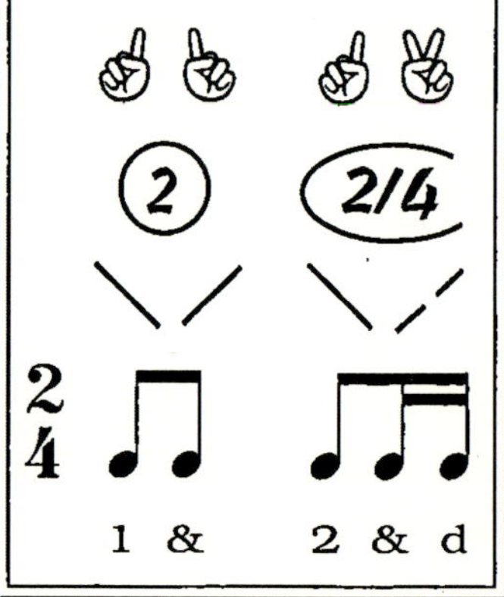

TABLE OF CONTENTS

LESSON 1 Rhythmic Association

Objectives

- Move foot (establish pulsation) and vocalize the number of fingers
- Counting is an optical illusion

Materials

Recorded music

Procedure

(Refer to HOW TO USE THE GAMES OF MUSIC pg. 5 prior to teaching these lessons)

Foot Movement

(If you do not use foot movement, establish your method of pulsation at this time)

1) Instruct the students to **imitate** your foot movement.
   - Instruct students to slide to the edge of their chair.
   - Instruct students to select either the left or right foot, leave the heal on the floor, and raise the front part of their foot.
   - Use a simple down and up pattern with your arms, hands and foot. (Form fist with each hand) Instruct students to imitate your **foot** when they think they can. Students **do not** imitate your sign language.
   - After everyone has joined, tap 7-8 additional beats.

2) Add recorded music and have the students tap their foot for several beats. Pulse 56-60

Rhythmic Association

1) Students move their foot and **count** the **number of fingers** raised on the directors hands. Indicate the sign language for ④ (first two fingers on each hand). Explain that "when your foot is **DOWN**, count the number of fingers raised on my **RIGHT** hand (2). When your foot is **UP**, count the number of fingers raised on my **LEFT** hand (2)." Have the students **begin** with foot tap only (fist on each hand). **Next,** add sign language and continue to say "1-2↘, 1-2↗". Students join in and say "1-2, 1-2" when they think they can. Students **do not** imitate your sign language.

2) Repeat the process for ②. Indicate the sign language (first finger of each hand) move foot , direct, and continue to say "1↘, 1↗". Students are to join when they can.

3) Repeat the process for ① ( ). **Do not** be concerned with how long they say "**1**".

4) **Review** each of the 3 subdivisions. (4-5 beats per subdivision). **Always** begin this process with **foot movement only**. After 3-4 beats of foot movement **add** the sign language and counting.

5) Next, have the students perform each of the 3 subdivisions; **2 beats** per subdivision.

6) Inform students that you are now going to **mix** all 3 subdivisions.
Give the following rhythmic sequence **with sign language**. (Do not write these number symbols on the board)

SEQUENCE: ④ ② ④ ① ④ ④ ①

After they perform the sequence, congratulate them and **illustrate** on the board what they just accomplished.

7) Students are to perform the sequence **again** as you point to the rhythms. Use the **sign language** as you point to the rhythm on the board.

8) Explain that counting is an **OPTICAL ILLUSION**. All there is to counting is finding out how many notes are on the **down beat** and how many are on the **up beat. ANYONE CAN DO IT!** INSTRUCT THE STUDENTS TO TURN TO PAGE 44 IN THEIR BOOKS AND COPY THE FOLLOWING ILLUSTRATION. (students are to use pages 44 - 48 for taking notes on new rhythmic concepts)

Counting Is An
Optical Illusion...
Anyone Can Do It!

Review

1) **The foot controls counting**
2) **Counting is an optical illusion**

Comments

- *STUDENTS DETERMINE THE SPEED AT WHICH YOU WILL INTRODUCE NEW MATERIAL.*
- *Do not be concerned, at this time, with those whose foot does not move exactly right.*
- *Why bother with recorded music? Recorded music acts as a metronome. Students enjoy it!*

LESSON 2 The Beat

Objectives

- Relationship of the foot to the beat
- Correct foot movement
- 3 qualities of a successful counter

Warm Up

1) Direct a simple down and up pattern for students to practice foot tap/pulsation.

2) Students count ④ ② ① by the number of fingers raised on director's hand.

Procedure

1) Explain and illustrate that sound = notes, silence = rests, and counting = foot.
2) Explain that when the foot moves **down and up 1 time**, it **represents 1 BEAT**. When the foot moves **down and stops,** it **represents 1/2 of a BEAT**. (The fact that an up beat is also 1/2 beat will be discussed at a later time). Illustrate the 3 functions of the foot.

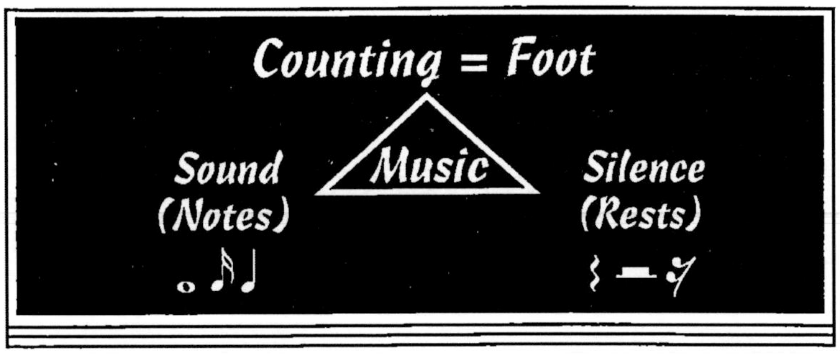

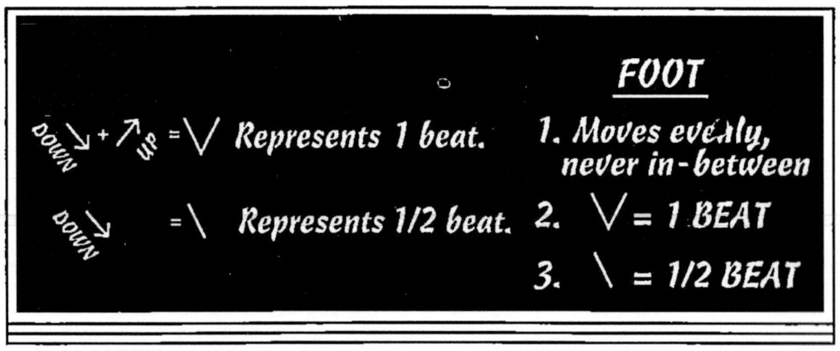

3) Move your foot down and up 3 1/2 times, leaving your foot in the down position when finished. Explain that even though they said, **"4"** in their head, it is only **3 1/2 beats** because there was not an **up beat**.
4) Demonstrate the difference between the foot moving **evenly** and the foot **"bouncing"**. Explain that when the foot bounces, it stays in the **up** position longer than the down position. The correct movement should be very **even.**
5) Move your foot down and up 3 times and ask the students **how many beats** that represented. (Make sure your foot **ends** in the **up** position) Use the same procedure for various numbers of beats.
6) Students practice the correct foot movement. Direct **without** sign language. To get the students started, use the command: "Foot in the **up** position - READY, AND, GO, AND, **DOWN** (↘), **UP** (↗)."
7) Students count **sign language** while concentrating on **correct** foot movement. Add music.
8) Explain that **successful** counters must have KNOWLEDGE, COORDINATION, plus one other trait. Inform them that the following contest will illustrate the **third** trait:

   Students slide to the edge of their chair. They are to move their foot down and up when you direct with your arms. When you **stop** directing, they are to **stop** their **foot**. If a student does not stop their foot, they are to slide to the back of the chair and keep their foot still. **Repeat** this process until only **one** student remains. Explain that **CONCENTRATION**, not knowledge or coordination, enabled them to win.

3 QUALITIES OF A SUCCESSFUL COUNTER:
Knowledge, Coordination, Concentration

Review

1) **Sound = notes; silence = rests; counting = foot/pulse**
2) **3 functions of the foot (moves evenly, never in-between; \/ =1 beat; \ =½ beat)**
3) **3 qualities of a successful counter (knowledge; coordination; concentration)**

LESSON 3 Subdivision

Objectives

- Terminology for ④ ② ①
- Definition for SUBDIVISION

Warm Up

1) **Students practice correct foot movement.**
2) **Students count fingers for ④ ② ①.**

Procedure

1) Write the word **divide** on the board and ask for other forms of that word, (division, dividend, divisor, etc.) When someone says the word **subdivision**, erase all words and write the word SUBDIVISIONS.
2) Relate the word SUBDIVISION to a **housing subdivision**. Explain that you take 1 big piece of land, **divide** it into smaller lots, build houses on the lots, and then sell the homes to people.
NEXT, explain that a **musical** subdivision works the same way, except you **divide 1 beat** (down and up) instead of 1 piece of land. The **1 beat** is **divided** into **equal** notes! Add the definition.

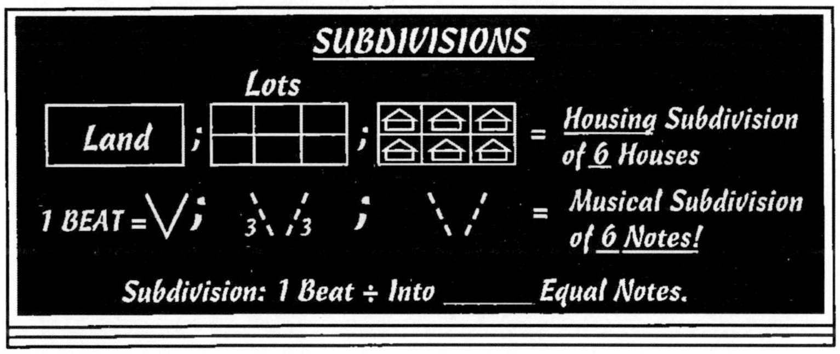

3) Students count the **number of fingers** for ④. 5 - 6 beats
4) Students count only 1 beat of a ④. **Make sure the foot freezes in the up position.** After the students count 3-4 **isolated** beats of ④, ask them, "How many numbers did you say on the down beat?" "How many numbers did you say on the up beat?" "How many is that all together?" "What musical subdivision would that be?" Compare to housing subdivisions. Explain that " ◯ " around a number indicates SUBDIVISION.

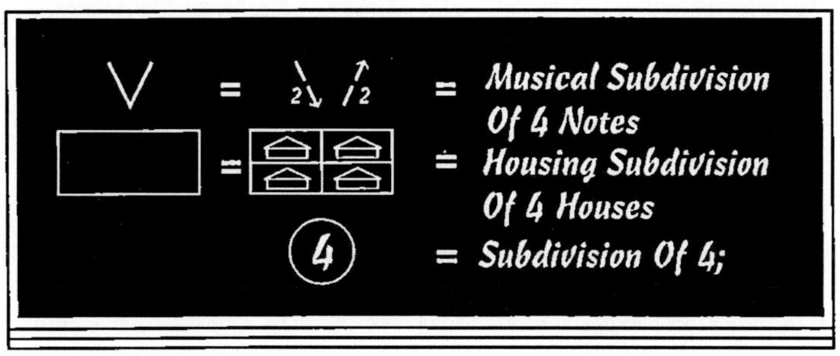

5) Change 1-2 (\ ), 1-2 (/) to the **correct** terminology. "From now on we will say **1-e, &-d**" instead of "1-2, 1-2". After illustrating, tap your foot, direct, count out loud, and have the students **join** you when they can using the **new** terminology. Next write 5-6 beats of ④ on the board for students to count. Point to each ④ **as they count** them. Explain they can now count ④ two different ways; **sign language** and **number symbols.**

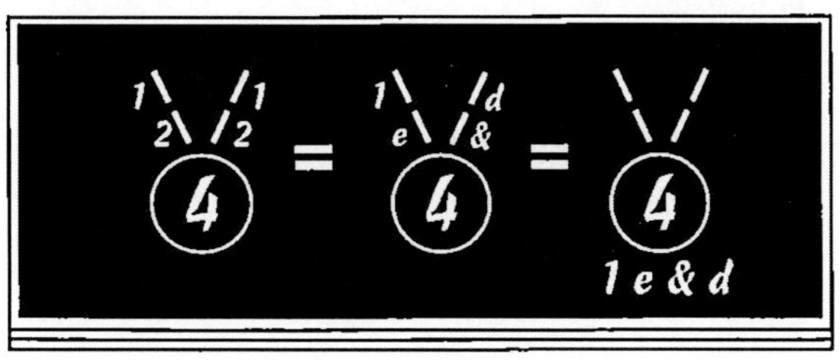

6) Use the same procedure to explain and illustrate ②. Count only **1 beat** of ②, and ask how many notes were on the **down beat** and how many were on the **up beat**. Change to the correct terminology.

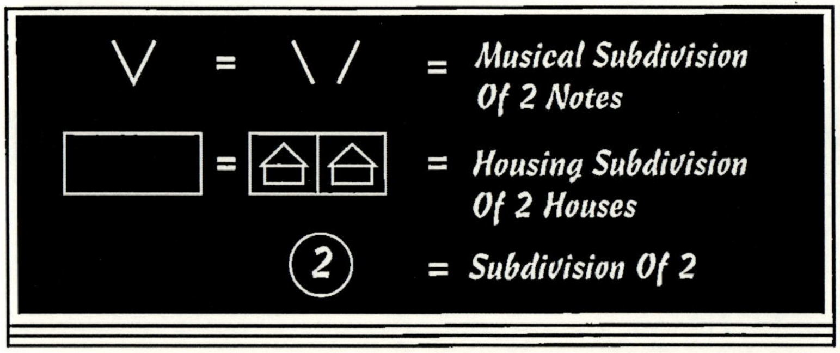

7) Students count ② with new terminology / **sign language**. Next, have the students count ② & ④. Start with 3-4 beats of ④, then 3-4 beats of ②. **KEEP THE TEMPO SLOW**. Finally switch back and forth between ② & ④ to internalize the new terminology.

8) **a)** Students count ② ④ with **number symbols**. **Group** several beats of ② ④ for students to count.
b) **Erase** and write a different rhythmic sequence that mixes ② ④.

10) Use the same procedure to explain and illustrate ①.

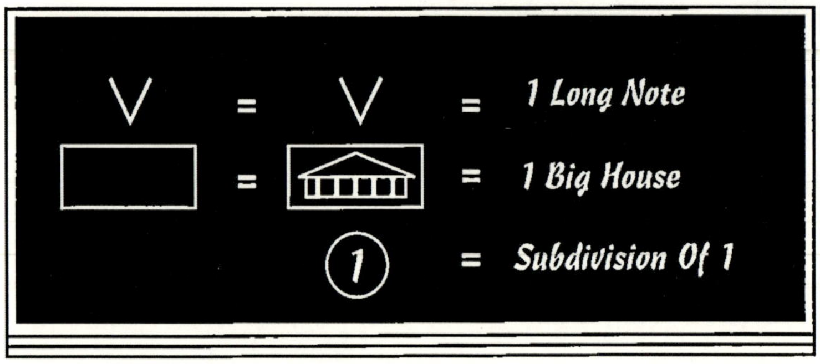

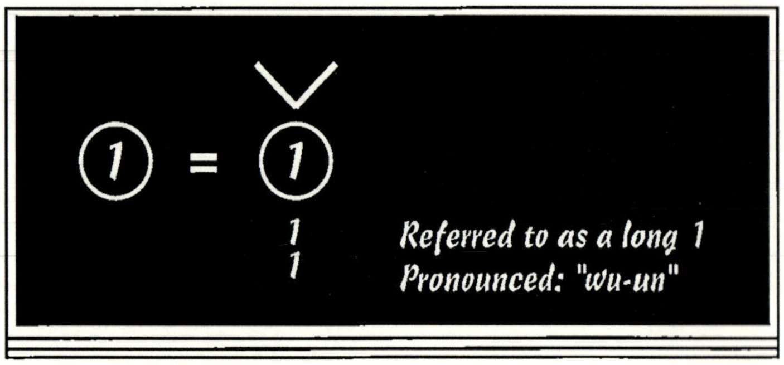

11) Students perform ④ ② ① with sign language. **GROUPED & MIXED**.

12) Students count ④ ② ① with number symbols. **GROUPED & MIXED**.

13) Apply the definition for SUBDIVISION to ④ ② ①. EX. ②: 1 BEAT ÷ INTO **2** = NOTES.

Review

1) **Definition for subdivision: one beat divided into __________ equal notes**
2) **Definition for ④, ②, ① (④ = "One beat divided into 4 equal notes", etc.)**
3) **A "◯" around a number represents SUBDIVISION.**
4) **New terminology for ④ ② ①. (1e-&d, 1-&, wu-un)**

Comments

- *When there is a breakdown in playing or sight reading, one must diagnose whether the problem was caused by KNOWLEDGE, COORDINATION, or CONCENTRATION. More often than not, the problem is **mis**diagnosed as KNOWLEDGE.*
- *For several days have the students stop their counting syllables on the **up beat** for the ①. This will help the students to internalize the **basic** concept for a note that lasts 1 beat. You can **lengthen** the ① later (style). REMIND STUDENTS THAT **ALL RHYTHMS** BEGIN ON **DOWN BEATS!***

LESSON 4 Sizzle

Objectives

- Add metronome to counting
- Sizzle

Warm Up

1) **Count ④ ② ① with sign language.**
2) **Count ④ ② ① with number symbols.**

Procedure

1) Explain that the metronome is a musicians best friend and that it keeps an **even** pulse/beat. Set the metronome so there is a "click" for the **down beat** and a "click" for the **up beat.** Students count sign language/number symbols with the metronome. ① **= 50.**
2) Demonstrate the sizzle. (Teeth almost touching, tongue behind the teeth to produce a "sssss" sound).
3) Give the sign language for ②, tap your foot, direct and sizzle several ②. Instruct the students to join you when they can. Make the two sizzles that represent "1-&" short.
4) Have the students sizzle **1 beat** of ②. (Make sure the foot freezes on the up). Ask how many sizzles were on the **down** beat and **up** beat. Explain and illustrate that since there was **1** on the **down** and **1** on the **up**, they sizzled a ②.

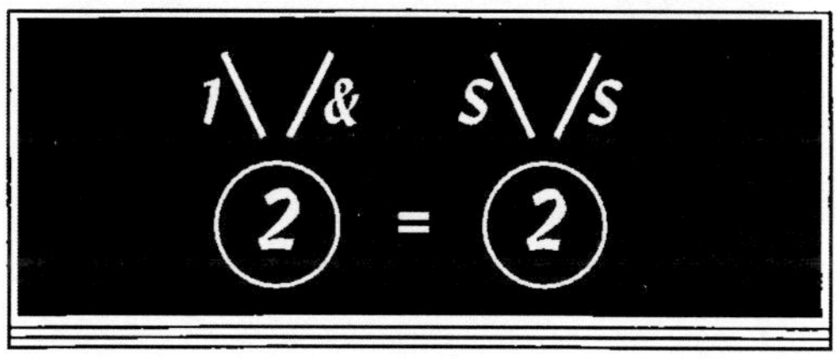

5) Students sizzle several beats of ② with number symbols. Instruct the students to "**scream** the counting syllables" **in their mind** as they sizzle the rhythm. Direct and move **your foot** down and up as you say the following command: " (↘) READY, (↗) AND, (↘) SIZZLE AND, (↗) SCREAM."
6) Use the same process for ④.
   - Students imitate directors sizzle and foot tap
   - Sizzle 1 beat of ④. Stop foot on the up beat
   - Students sizzle several ④ with sign language
   - Mix ② & ④ with sign language
   - Students sizzle several ④ with number symbols
   - Mix ② & ④ with number symbols
   - DO NOT be concerned with **legato** style at this time
   - Count/sizzle from student text, pgs. 4 & 5

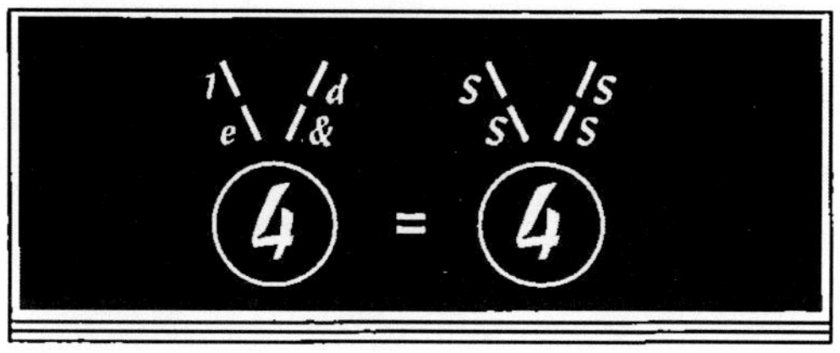

Review

1) **The sizzle represents the length of a note**
2) **Keep the sizzles short for ④ ② and long for ①**

Comments

- *Sizzle vs. clapping. Clapping requires physical movement that is never utilized during ones performance of a musical instrument. The physical aspects of clapping create other coordination problems that are unnecessary and adds to the problems of counting education. (An exemption would be the percussionists). Sizzling is internal where as clapping is external. Sizzling utilizes muscles from the waist/abdomen extending all the way through the head. Orchestra students should add shadow bowing.*

LESSON 5 Recognition Of Notes

Procedure

1) **a)** Draw a 64th note and a whole note and ask how many different "things" the first note has that the second note does not have. **b)** Draw another whole note and add the 6 different "things", **one at a time.**

2) Inform the students that in music there is a **magic** number and that number is "2".
a) Draw a whole note and ask how many symbols they see. **b)** Add "1 " and another whole note (the additional whole note will become the half note). **c)** Explain that every time you **add** a "thing" to the note, you multiply the number of the **previous** note with the "2". **d)** Continue this process until you arrive at the 64th note.

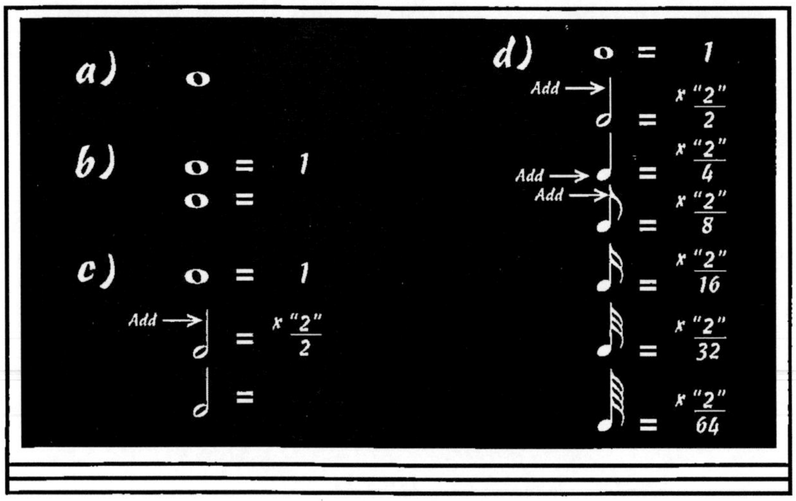

3) **Erase** all the "2", "x", and "__" leaving the notes and numbers. Point to the number 64 by the sixty fourth note and explain that the **name** of the note sounds like its number. Explain and illustrate all flagged notes. Next, explain that when you run out of flags, you run into money. Refer to the whole note and associate it with 1 **whole** dollar. Follow this procedure for half note and quarter note.

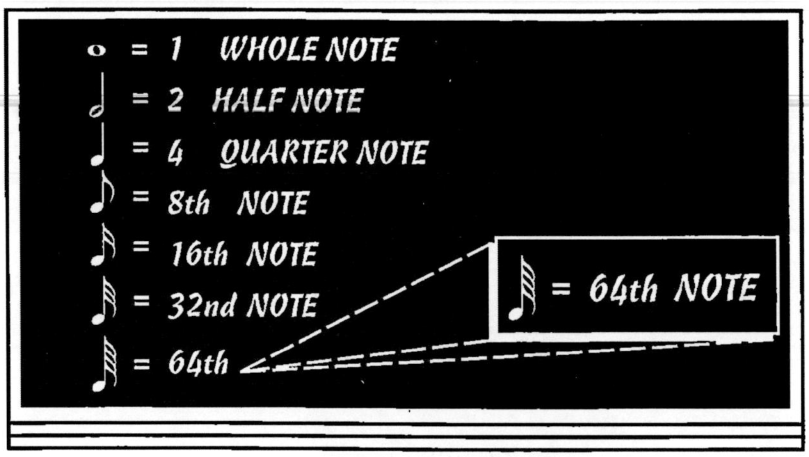

Review

1) Non-flagged notes; 𝅝 𝅗𝅥 ♩ - their names are spelled out

Flagged notes; 𝅘𝅥𝅮 𝅘𝅥𝅯 𝅘𝅥𝅰 𝅘𝅥𝅱 - their names sound like their number

2) 32nd note has 3 flags   64th note has 4 flags

LESSON 6 The Games of Music ①

Objectives

- Purpose of a time signature
- Bottom number of a time signature
- Recognition of ① by notes

Warm Up

1) **Count/sizzle rhythms with sign language.**
2) **Count/sizzle a rhythmic sequence from board using number symbols.**
3) ***Count from student text page 4.***

Procedure

1) **a)** Write a number sequence on the board for the students to count. Explain that in music we do not count by numbers but by **notes.** "Our next step is to assign notes to the number symbols. How do we start that process?" Explain that at the **beginning** of **every** song they will find a **time signature.** It is the time signature that starts the process of assigning notes to the number symbols.

2) **b)** Explain and illustrate the fact that the **top number** of a time signature is not important (at this time). It is the **bottom** number that tells us the ***GAME*** and how to begin assigning the notes to the number symbols. (show them 3 different songs, each with a different number in the bottom of the time signature)

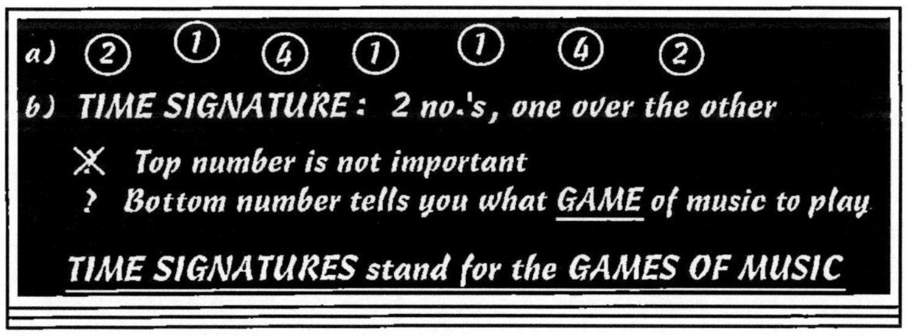

3) **a)** Write a ? and re-explain that it represents the **top number. b)** Next, **add** the **order** of numbers used to teach the names of notes. Explain and illustrate that these **bottom numbers** represent the **GAMES** of music. **c)** Isolate GAMES 1, 2, 4, 8, & 16. **d)** Ask the students for an observation concerning the bottom numbers (numbers used to learn the names of notes). **Add** the notes by the numbers and explain the **bottom number** is not really a number, but a **"note in disguise"**. **e)** Isolate various time signatures. **f)** Explain that the bottom number of a time signature will tell them "3 things". The first "2 things" are the **GAME** and a **"NOTE IN DISGUISE"**.

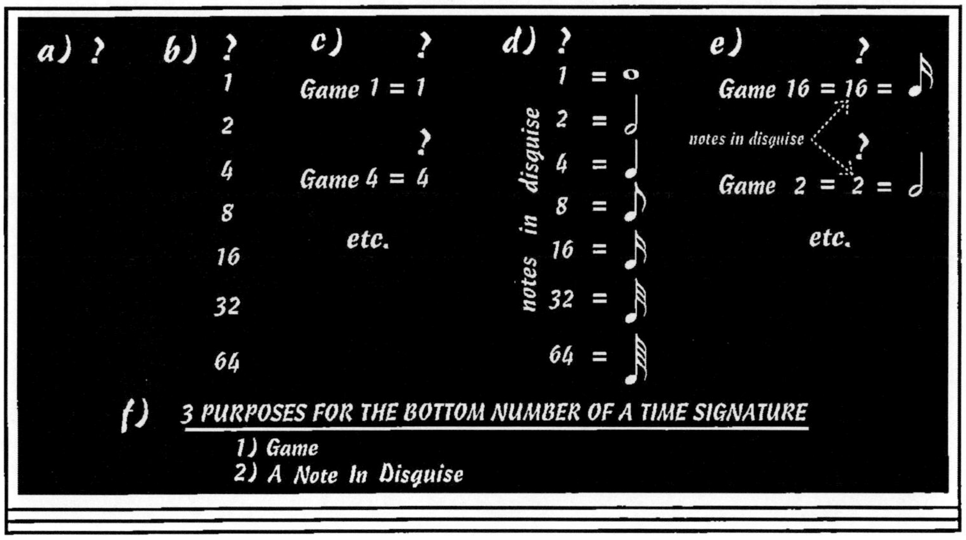

4) Explain that the **third** purpose is the most **IMPORTANT. IN EACH GAME THE NOTE IN DISGUISE ALWAYS REPLACES THE ① 's.** Illustrate some GAMES in this order: time signature, GAME, note in disguise, ①.

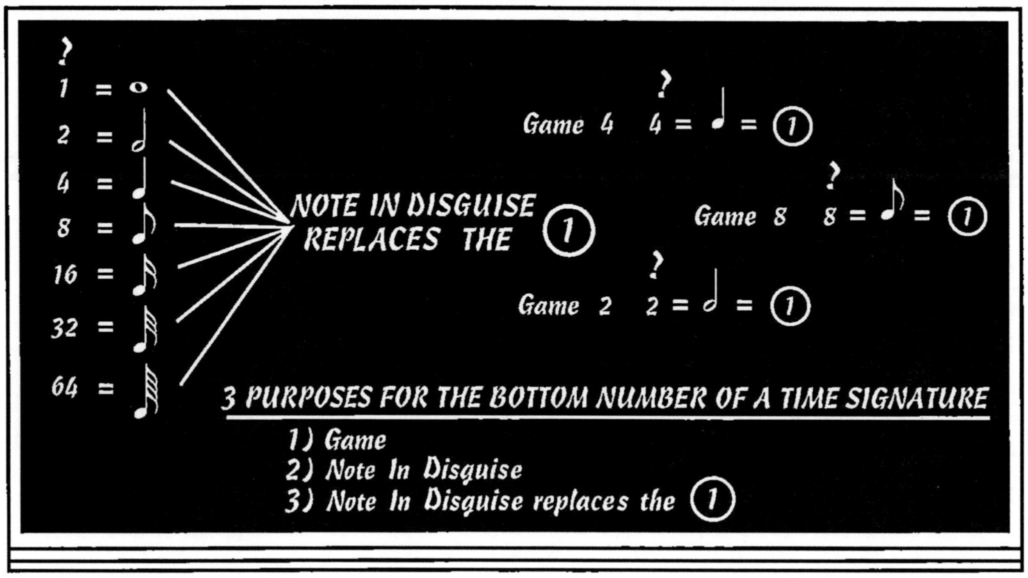

5) **a)** Write a rhythmic sequence for the students to count. **b) After** they have counted the sequence, add a time signature, ask for the 3 purposes and illustrate as follows. **c) Change** the 1's inside of the circles to the correct **notation**. Have the students count the sequence again, emphasizing the fact that they can now count the ① by **notes** in addition to sign language and number symbols! (Draw the students attention to the fact that the **4** in the **bottom** of the time signature and the **4** in the ④ do not indicate the same information)

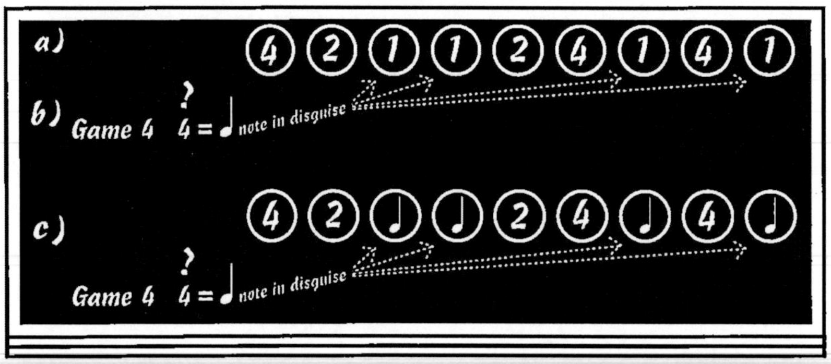

6) Two important question to emphasize at this time; "Why does music require a time signature"? (To find the note in disguise) "Which **number symbol** does the note in disguise **ALWAYS** replace"? (①)
Repeat the above illustration for other GAMES.

Review

1) **Time signatures = the GAMES of music**
2) **Time signature is located at the beginning of a song, and has 2 numbers**
3) **The top number is not important, the bottom number tells us "3 things":**
   A) Game B) The Note In Disguise C) The Note In Disguise ALWAYS replaces the ①

LESSON 7 Note Values ②

Objectives

- Note value for ②
- Recognition of notes for ②
- Count/sizzle notation for ② ①

Warm Up

1) **Count/sizzle basic rhythms with sign language.**
2) **Count/sizzle a rhythmic sequence from the board using number symbols.**
3) **Add a time signature for the rhythmic sequence and have the entire class give the 3 purposes for the bottom number of the time signature. Write their answers to the left of the time signature.**
4) **Substitute the note value for the ① 's and have the students count/sizzle.**
5) **Student text pg. 4.**

Procedure

1) "Now that we know how to find the notes for the ①, how do we find the 2 notes for the ②?" **a)** Instruct the students to turn to page 45 and copy the following illustration. Draw a 64th note and its fraction on the board and explain that it is a "lonely " 64th note. **b)** To make it feel better you add another 64th note. Add the other fraction and show that the 2 fractions equal 1 - 32nd note (a lonely 32th note). Continue this process until you arrive at the whole note. Draw the notes **larger** as you approach the whole note.

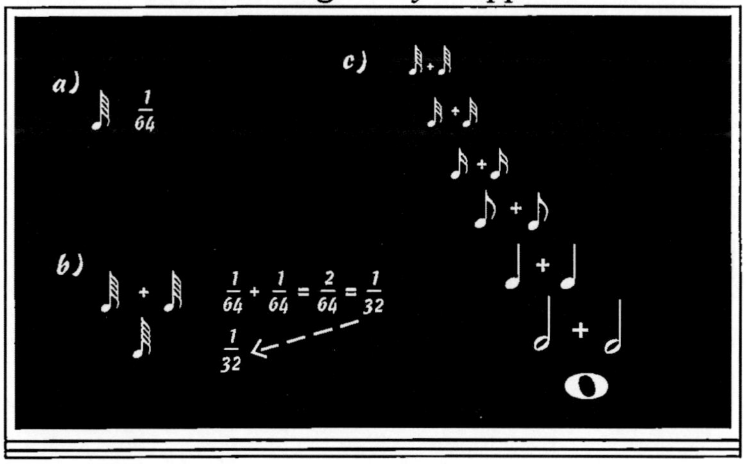

2) Point to different notes and ask what **2** notes would equal that note. Refer students to their **note value charts** locted on the inside back cover of their book
3) **a)** Place a time signature on the board and ask for the **3 purposes**. **b)** Place their answers to the left. **c)** After the **note in disguise** has been established, ask what **2** notes would equal that note. **d)** Next, draw a circle around the note in disguise. **e)** Explain that since the **right** side equals the left side, you can also circle the **right** side. Since the note on the left side must be performed in **1 beat**, the **2** notes on the **right** side must be performed in **1 beat** as well. **f)** The students have discovered how to find the 2 notes that replace the ②'s. Repeat this process for other GAMES.

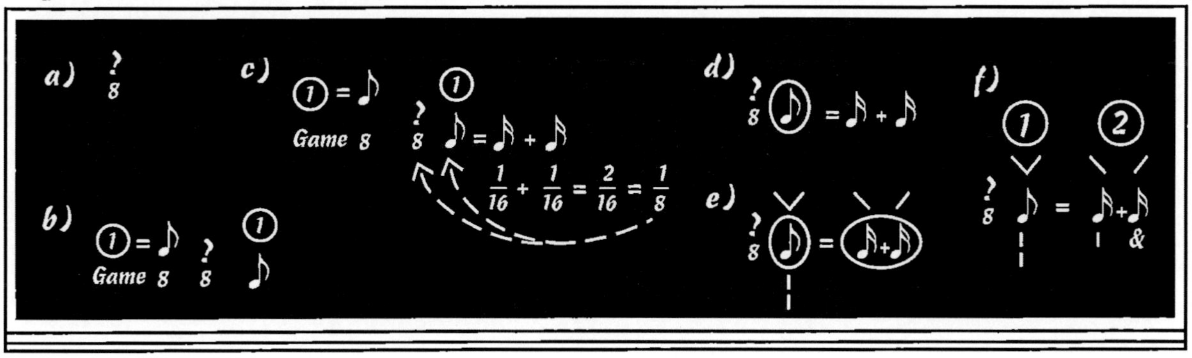

4) Apply the definition for ②. One beat, divided into 2 equal notes.

5) **a)** Write a rhythmic sequence using ④ ② ① for students to count/sizzle. **b)** Add a time signature and ask the students for the **note in disguise** and the the **2 notes** that would equal the note in disguise. Draw the arrows from the notes to the appropriate subdivision and add the RULES to the left. **c)** Next, substitute the **note in disguise** for the ①'s and the note values for the ②'s and have the students re-count/sizzle.

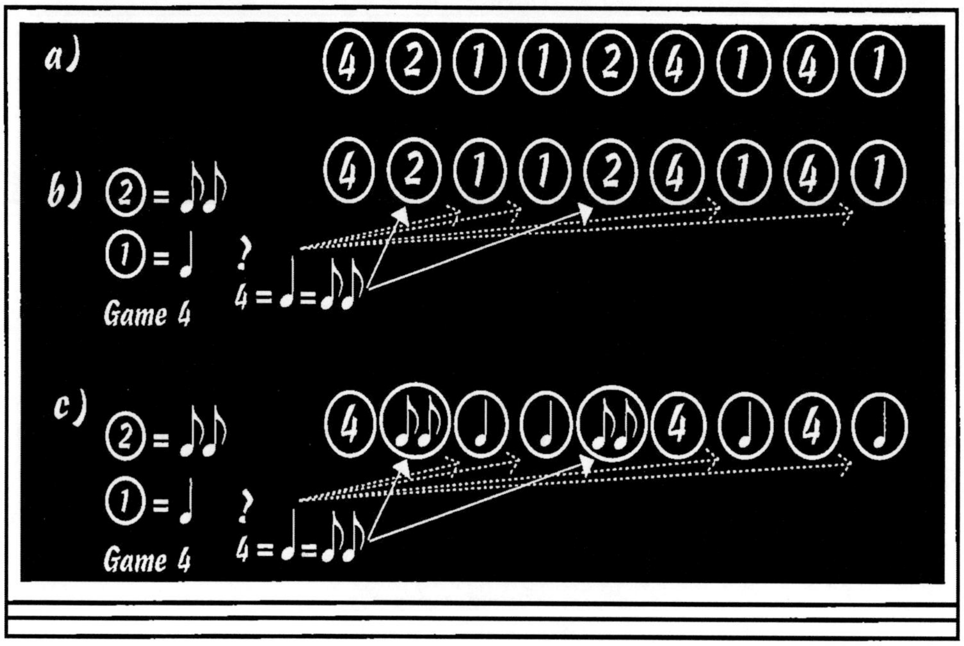

Internalization

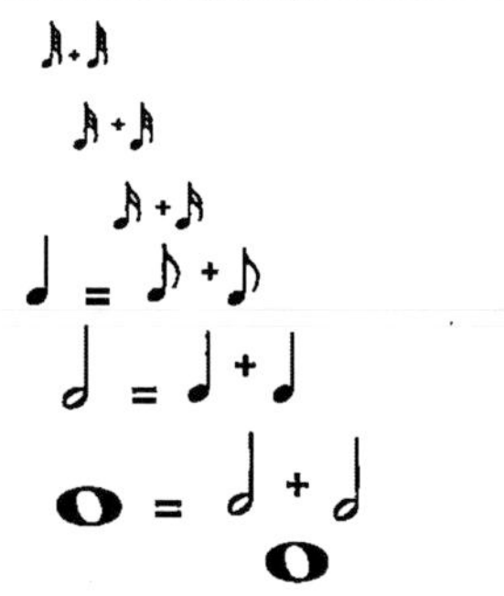

BOARD GAME

② = ? ② =

① = ① =

GAME = GAME =

2 students go to the board. The teacher chooses a GAME by adding a bottom no. to the time signature. The student who writes the correct answers first, wins.

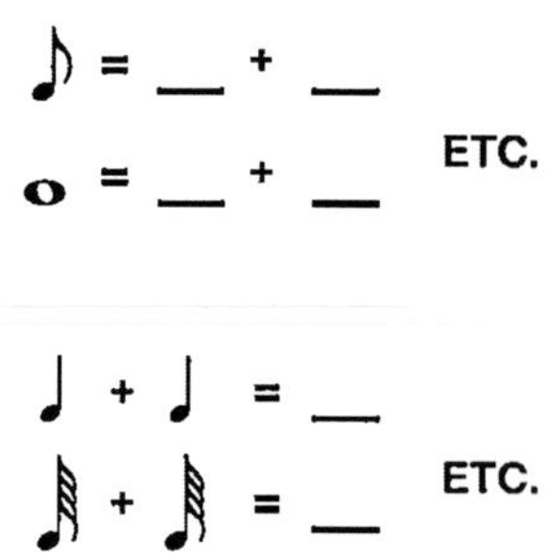

Daily Drill #1	Daily Drill #2
Director says a note, student quickly tells what 2 notes equal that note. ex. Director: "Quarter note!" Student: "2 eighth notes"	Director: "What tells you the ① ?" Student: "Note in disguise/time signature note" Director: "How do you find the ② ?" Student: "The 2 notes that = the note in disguise/ time signature note/①."

Review

1) Definition for ②: one beat divided into 2 equal notes
2) Note values for ②
3) How do you find the ②? (2 notes that equal the note in disguise/ time signature note /①)

Comments

- ***Do not** go to ④ note values until ② note values have been internalized. Note values are the most difficult concepts for students to grasp. Drill students **daily** on their note values.*
- *Do not flood their minds with the **entire** note value chart at this time. Wait until ② and ④ are internalized. Note Value Charts are located inside the back cover of **student text.***
  *When the note values for ② require flagged notes, **do not** flag them together! Keep them **individual**. Do the same for ④ until these 2 subdivisions are internalized.*

LESSON 8 Note Values ④

Objectives

- Note values for ④
- Recognition of notes for ④
- Count / Sizzle / sing notation for ④ ② ①

Warm Up

1) **Director says a note, students respond with the 2 notes that equal that note.**
2) **Count/sizzle basic rhythms with sign language.**
3) **Count/sizzle a rhyhmic sequence from the board using number symbols.**
4) **Add a time signature, students give the 3 purposes and what 2 notes equal the main note. Write answers to the left of time signature.**
5) **Substitute the correct note values, one subdivision at a time, and have students count/sizzle each time. Select a pitch and have students sing the rhythm.**
6) **Student text.**

Procedure

1) **a)** Draw the note value chart for ②. **b)** Refer to the **2 half notes** and explain that since the first half note equals 2 quarter notes, the **other** half note would also equal 2 quarter notes. Continue this process until you arrive at **four** 64th notes (**do not** complete the entire note value chart at this time). Use fractions to explain.

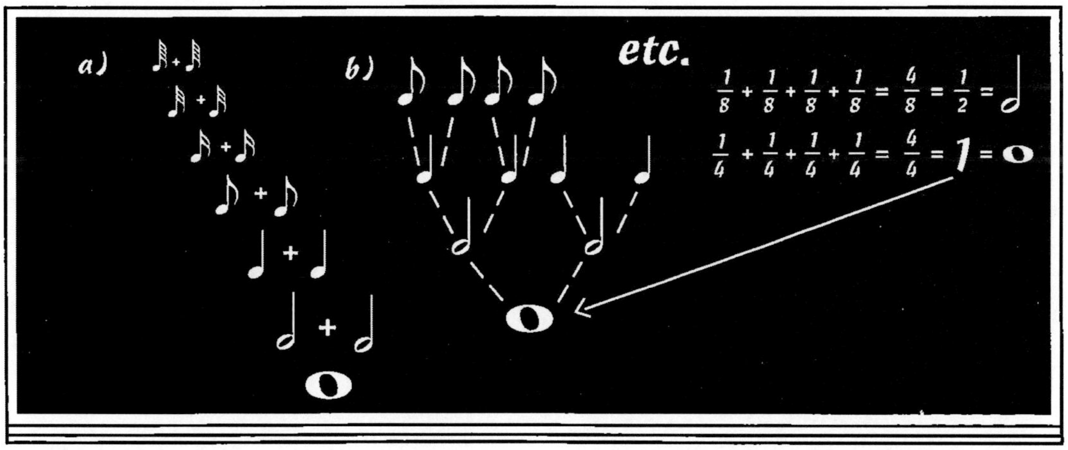

2) Point to a particular note and ask what **2 notes** and what **4 notes** would equal that note.

3) Explain and illustrate the relationship of ④ to the main note. **a)** Begin with the time signature, then add the RULES to the left. Use the same process to explain and illustrate the other games.

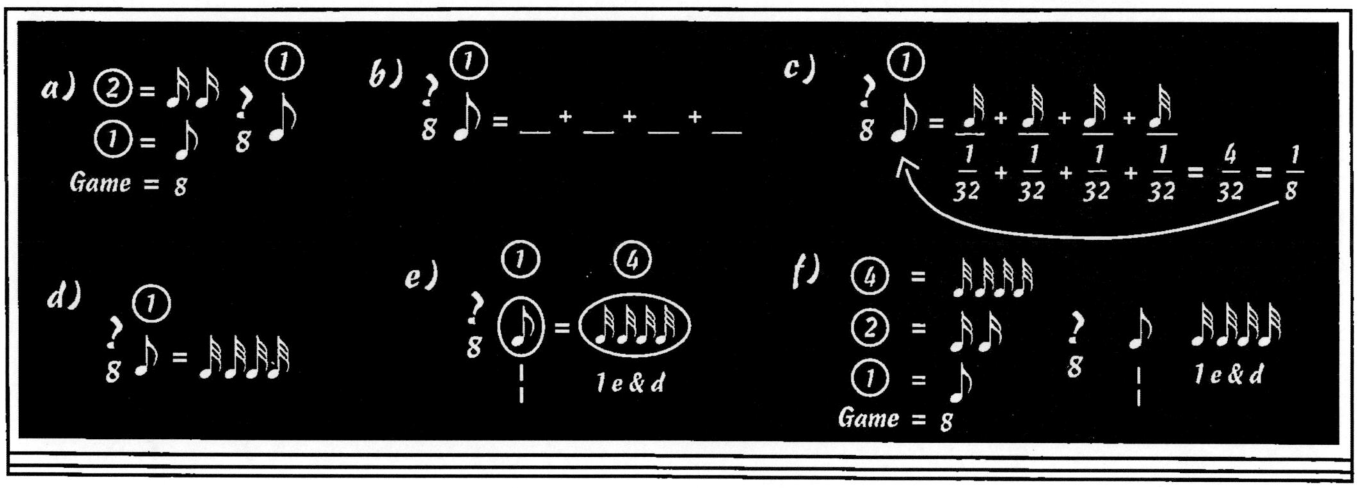

4) Definition for ④. One beat divided into 4 equal notes

5) **a)** Write a rhythmic sequence using **number symbols** for students to count/sizzle. **b) Add** a time signature and ask for the **GAME** and **the note in disguise**, write the note in disguise to the right of the time signature. Ask what **2** notes equal the note in disguise, ask what **4** notes equal the note in disguise and write their answers to the right and rules to the left. Draw the arrows from the notes to the appropriate subdivision. c) Substitute the correct **note** values, **beginning with the** ① and have the students count/sizzle the rhythmic sequence. Illustrate in all GAMES.

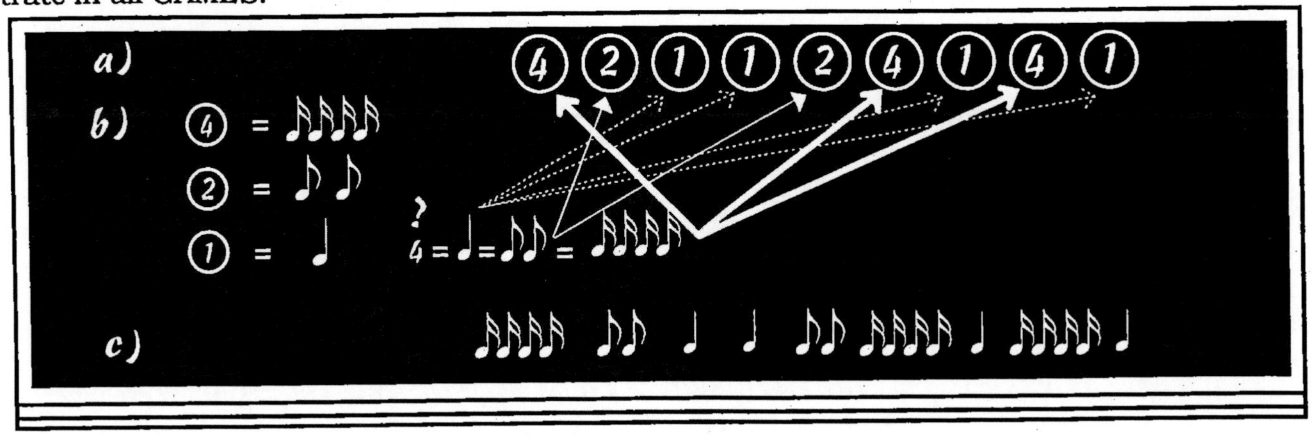

6) Instruct students to complete the chalkboards on page 6. **Once students are able to perform rhythms on their instrument**, remind them to simply, ""PLAY what you SAY". If they say "1-e,&-d", they articulate "ta-ta-ta-ta" on their instrument. Students complete NOTE VALUE CHART #1 and the first three columns of #2 on page 39.

Internalization

Daily Drill #1

Director: "half note!"
Student: "2 quarter notes, 4 eight notes!"
(use this process for all GAMES. You are stating the note in disguise, students are stating the answers for the notes that replace the ② & ④)

BOARD GAME

Director adds the botttom no. 2 Students compete for answers

	?	
④ =		④ =
② =		② =
① =		① =
GAME =		GAME =

Daily Drill #2

Director: "what do you need to replace the numbers with notes"? (students: time signature)
Director: "top or bottom number"? (students: bottom)
Director: "is it a number"? (students:no)
Director: "it is a "? (students:note in disguise)
Director: "the note in disquise always replaces"? (students: the 1's)
Director: "how do you find the 2's and 4's"? (students: the note value chart)

STUDENT TEXT: When students count the notation on odd numbered pages, use this procedure:

1. "What is the note in disguise"?
2. "How many subdivisions of 1's, 2's, etc. (current)
3. Students tell you the name of each rhythm ("tie 2, subdivision of 4, combination2/4. etc.") in order
4. Students count each rhythm out loud. For exercises that do not have measures, students begin each rhythm with "1".
5. Students perform the exercise on their instrument

Review

1) Definition for ④: one beat divided into 4 equal notes
2) Note values for ④
3) How do you find the ④ ? (The note value chart; the 4 notes that equal the note in disguise)

Comments

- *Changing the TIME SIGNATURE **does not** change the **rhythm, ONLY WHAT IT LOOKS LIKE!***
- *Go to the next step when 90+ % of the students have internalized the lesson. **More time** spent at the beginning stages will **save time** in the future. Skip Lesson 9 andcontinue with **Tie** rhythms in Lesson 10*
- *When you switch your emphasis to tonal production, **DO NOT DROP COUNTING ALL TOGETHER.** A **DAILY** review of sign language, number symbols, and notation can be reinforced in less than 3-4 minutes.*

LESSON 9 Note Values ③ ⑥ ⑤ - ⑮

Objectives

- Recognition ③ & ⑥ through sign language, number symbols, notation for GAMES 2,4, and FAST $\frac{6}{8}$
- Recognition of ⑤, ⑦, ⑨, ⑪, ⑬, ⑮ through number symbols, notation

Warm Up

1) **Count/sizzle/sing/play basic rhythms with sign language.**
2) **Count/sizzle/sing/play a rhythmic sequence from the board using number symbols.**
3) **Notate the sequence, erase the number symbols, then count/sizzle/sing/play.**
4) **Student text.**

Procedure

1) Tap your foot, perform the ③, and instruct the students to join you when they can.
2) Explain and illustrate the number symbols for ③. Use the definition for **subdivision** in your explanation.

3) Students count/sizzle several beats of ③ through number symbols.

NOTE: If you introduce ③ in GAME 4, skip to procedure number 8) at this time.

4) **a)** Write the following rythmic sequence. **Add** the time signature and have the students count it in **SLOW** 6/8. **Gradually** increase the tempo until you reach a speed that is awkward to direct. **b)** Explain and illustrate that instead of directing **6 fast beats** per measure, you can accomplish the same rhythm by thinking a ③ with **2 beats** per measure. This method of counting is called FAST 6/8.

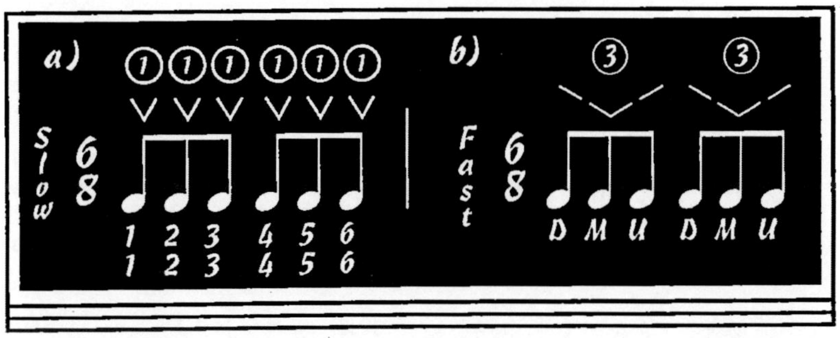

5) Explain and illustrate that by **tying** 3 eighth notes together you find the **NOTE IN DISGUISE**. The 8 in the bottom number of the time signature will stand for a dotted quarter note.

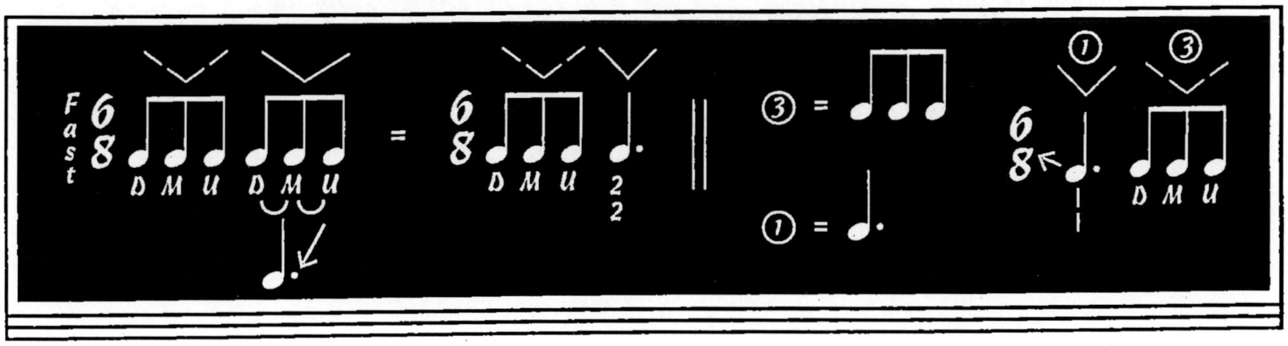

6) **a)** Write several ①'s & ③'s for students to count/sizzle/sing/play. **b)** Add a time signature, RULES to the left, notate, and instruct the students to re-count/sizzle/sing/play.

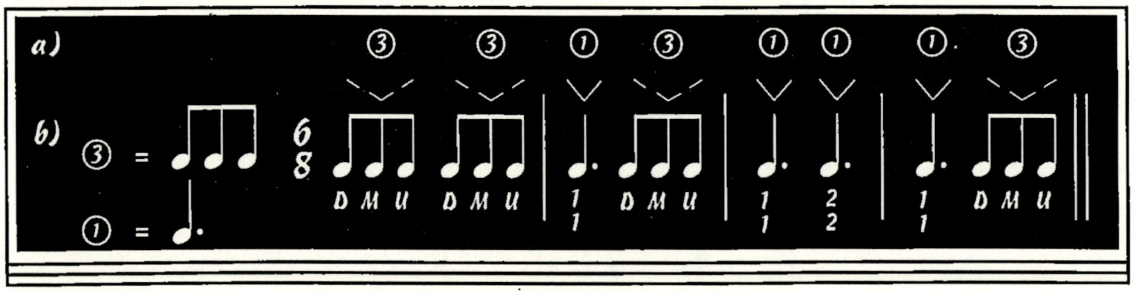

7) Student text pgs. 32 & 33. NOTE VALUE CHART #9, pg. 42.
8) Explain and illustrate the notation for ③ in **GAMES 4 & 2**. Looks like a ②, just **3** of them. The number "3" will normally appear above or below the rhythm.

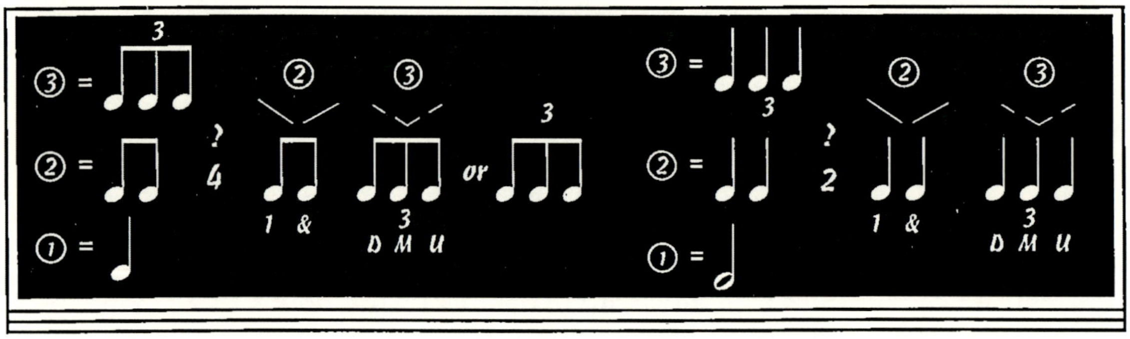

9) Mix ③ with all current rhythms. Add a time signature, RULES to the left, notate, and have students count/sizzle/sing/play. **NOTE:** Make sure the students' foot returns to a **snappy, never in-between** movement when counting ② ④ (2/4) etc.
10) Illustrate and compare ③ to (4/2). The most common problem of a ③ is to **rush** the **first** 2 notes.

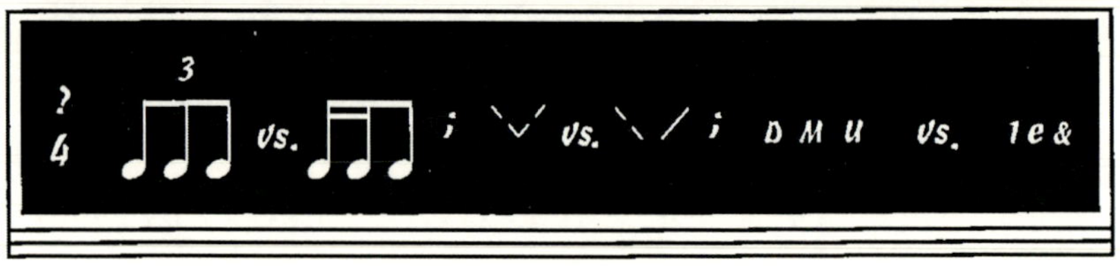

11) Student text pgs. 30 & 31. NOTE VALUE CHART #6, pg. 41.

Note Values ⑥

1) Students imitate your sizzle through sign language. (first three fingers of each hand).
2) **a)** Explain that each eighth note from the ③ is divided into two sixteenth notes. **b)** The result is six sixteenth notes; **3** on the **down** beat and **3** on the **up** beat. **c)** In FAST 6/8 it is usually easier to count "1,2,3,4,5,6". **d)** In GAMES **4 & 2** the notation for ⑥ looks the same as ④, just **6** of them. The number "6" will normally appear above or below the rhythm.

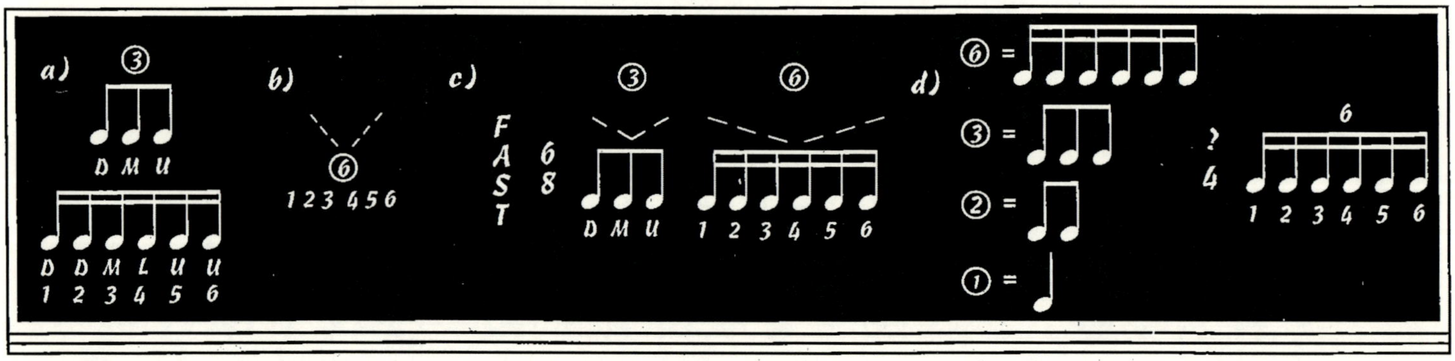

3) Mix ⑥ with all current rhythms. Add a time signature, RULES to the left, notate, and have students count/sizzle/sing/play.
4) Student text pg. 36. NOTE VALUE CHART #11, pg. 43. GAMES 2 & 4 located on CHART #6, pg. 41.

Note Values ⑤ ⑦

1) Explain that the notation for ⑤ & ⑦ looks like the notation for ④, just more of them. Some publishers will add a "5" or "7" above or below the rhythm. The **"7"** is pronounced **"sev"**.

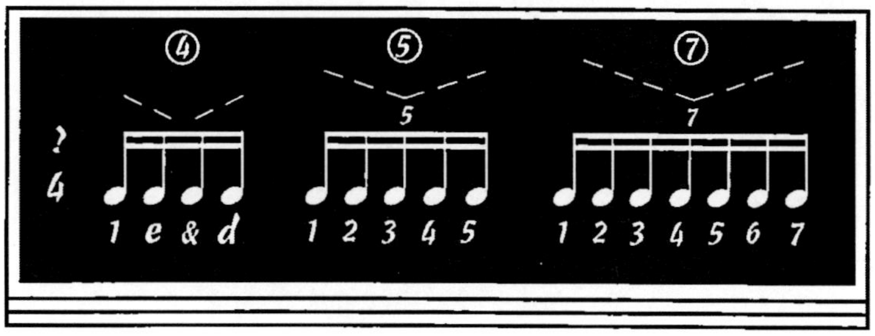

Note Values ⑨ - ⑮

1) Explain that the notation for ⑨ ⑩ ⑪ ⑫ ⑬ ⑭ ⑮ looks like the notation for ⑧, just more of them. Some publishers will place the specified number above or below the note.

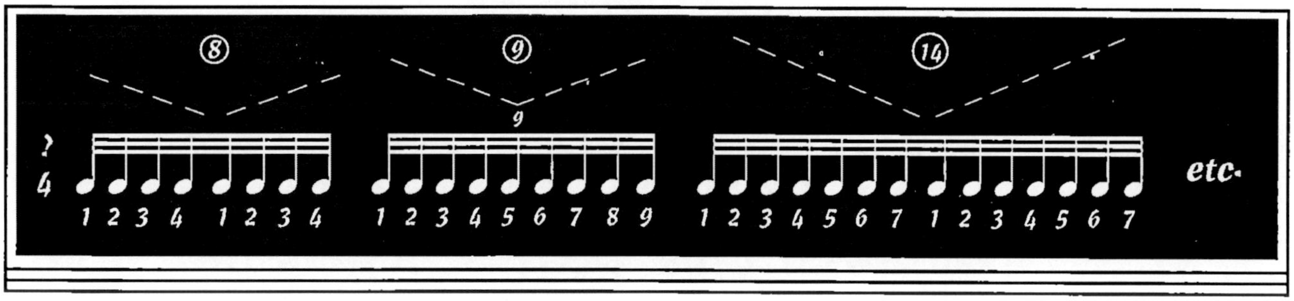

Review

1) **Counting syllables (③ Down-Mid-Up. ⑥ 1-2-3-4-5-6)**
2) **In FAST 6/8 the bottom "8" of the time signature stands for the dotted quarter note**
3) **The subdivision of ③ looks like the ②**
4) **The subdivision of ⑥ looks like the ④**
5) **The subdivisions of ⑤ & ⑦ looks like the ④**
6) **The subdivisions of ⑨ through ⑮ looks like the ⑧**

Comments

- *DO NOT INTRODUCE ③ UNTIL LATE IN THE YEAR. ⑥ WILL PROBABLY BE INTRODUCED DURING THE SECOND YEAR OF BAND.*
- *Say the syllables for ③ very "long" using a* ***mono tone****, like a robot.*
- *Explain that the foot will have a* ***smoother*** *feel while counting ③ rhythms.*
  Make sure the foot ***returns*** *to* ***snappy, never in-between*** *for ②, ④, 2/4 etc.*
- *When it is time to keep track of each beat within the measure, count ③ as follows:*

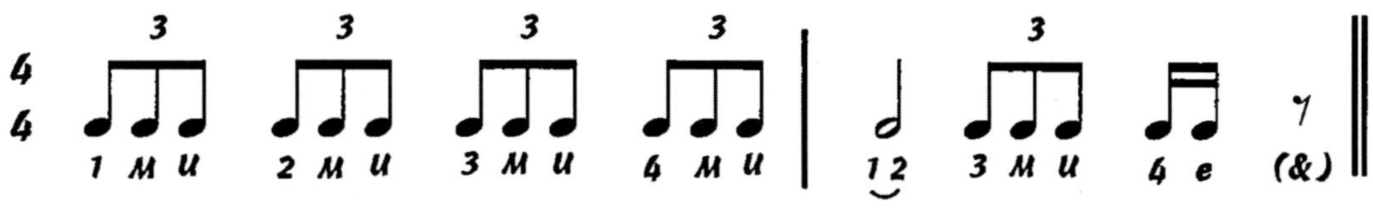

LESSON 10 Tie Rhythms & The Dot

Objectives

- Definition of TIE RHYTHMS
- Recognition of TIES through sign language, number symbols, notation
- FROM THIS POINT ON, DO NOT ILLUSTRATE IN GAMES 1 & 16

Warm Up

1) **Count/sizzle/sing/play basic rhythms with sign language.**
2) **Count/sizzle/sing/play a rhythmic sequence from the board using number symbols.**
3) **Notate the sequence, erase the number symbols, then count/sizzle/sing/play.**
4) **After ‿2‿ & ‿4‿ have been internalized, occasionally begin the class period with notation and have the students give you the number symbols.**
5) **Student text.**

Procedure

1) Explain that up to now all rhythms had to be performed within **1 beat**.

2) Ask if it is possible to have a note that lasts **longer** than 1 beat. If the students have been playing whole notes and half notes in their method books, you can relate this concept to their book.

3) Direct, tap your foot, sizzle ‿2‿ and instruct the students to join you when they can.

4) Direct their attention to the fact that their foot tapped **2 times** per sizzle. Explain and illustrate that you **tie** **2** ①'s to get ‿2‿. In music you "‿" rather than "+". Pronounced: "wu-un-two-oo".

5) Explain the sign language (touch your thumbs together) for ‿2‿. Have the students count/sizzle/sing several ‿2‿ rhythms. **After** they count by sign language, write 5-6 ‿2‿'s on the board for the students to count. Have students memorize the definition for TIE rhythms.

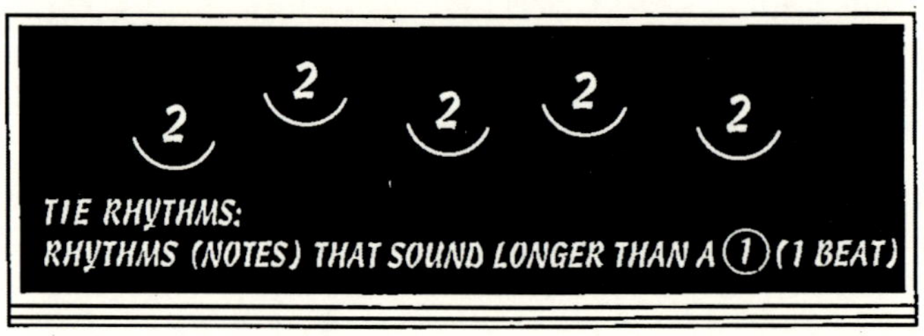

6) Students count/sizzle/sing/play a rhythmic sequence using ‿2‿ ① ② & ④.

7) Explain and illustrate the note that would represent ◡2◡ in various GAMES. **Always** point to the "◡" the "2" and the **bottom** number of the time signature as you explain. Reinforce that all you do is **TIE THE MAIN NOTE OF THE GAME**. Illustrate in all GAMES.

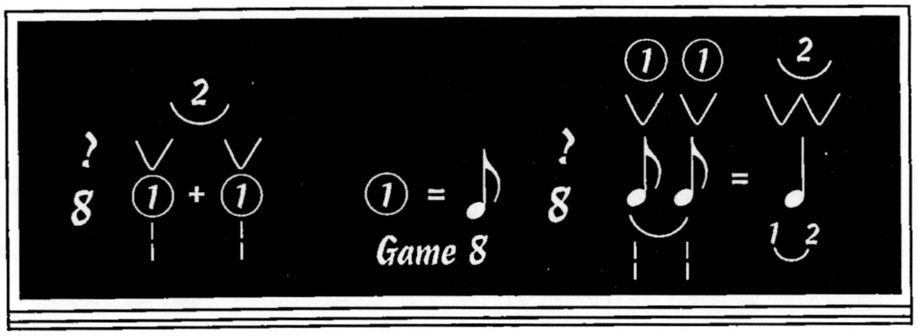

8) Mix ◡2◡ with all current rhythms. Add a time signature, RULES to the left, notate **1 RULE** at a time, and have the students count/sizzle/sing/play **each time**.

9) Student text pgs. 8 & 9. NOTE VALUE CHART #2, pg. 39.

10) Use the same procedure for ◡4◡ . Pronounced: "wu-un-two-oo-three-e-four-or" Illustrate the note values for a ◡4◡ rhythm. Notate ◡4◡ in all GAMES.

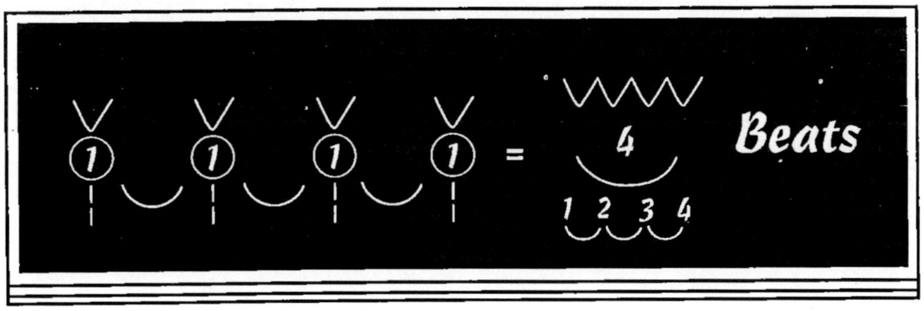

11) Mix ◡4◡ current rhythms, add a time signature, RULES to the left, notate **1 RULE** at a time, and have students count/sizzle/sing/play each time.

12) Student text pgs. 8 & 9. NOTE VALUE CHART #2, pg. 39.

"THE DOT"

1) **a)** Illustrate the 5 dotted half note. **First**, explain that a dot is a note **without** a stem or flag. **Next**, explain that the "dot note" is **1/2 the size** of the note it **follows**. **Finally**, explain that the "dot note" is **tied** to the note it **follows**. **b)** Inform the students that 95% of the time they will see a single dot. On occasion they will see a double dotted note.

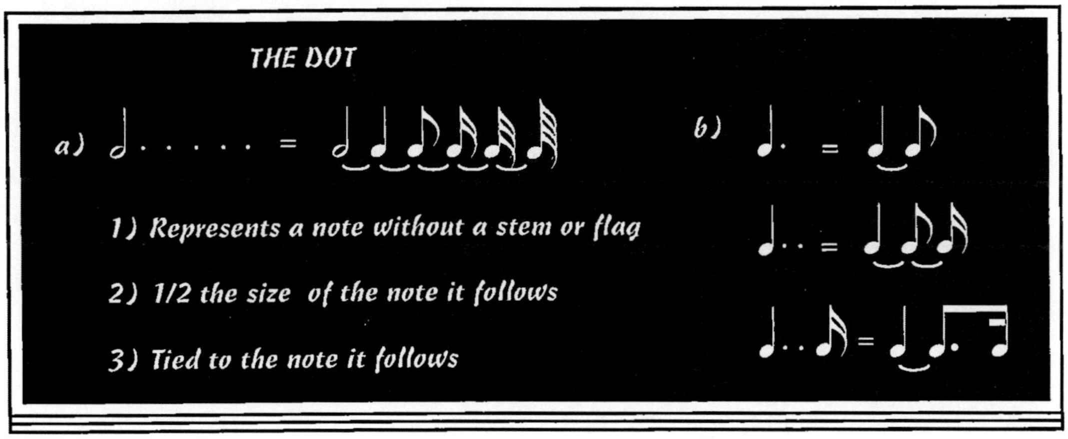

2˙ (3)

1) Explain that up to this point our TIE rhythms have lasted for 2 or 4 beats. Ask if it would be possible to have a note that lasted for **3** beats. Illustrate for all GAMES.

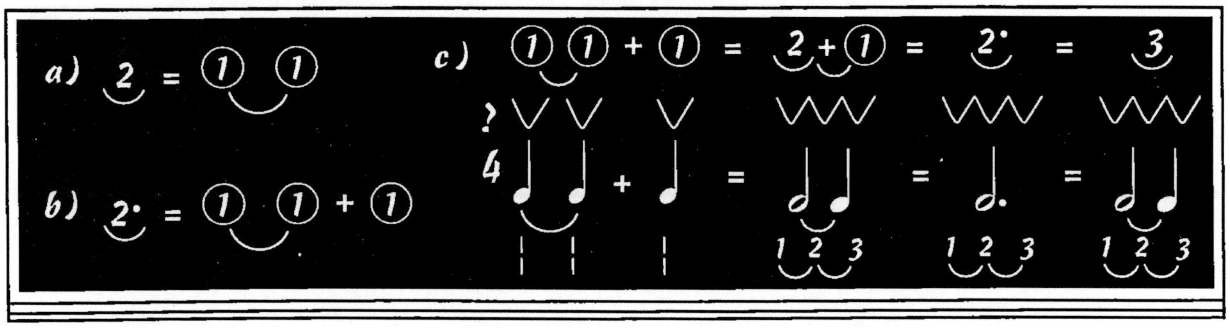

2) Explain and illustrate how the **time signature** effects the **length** of the dot/note.

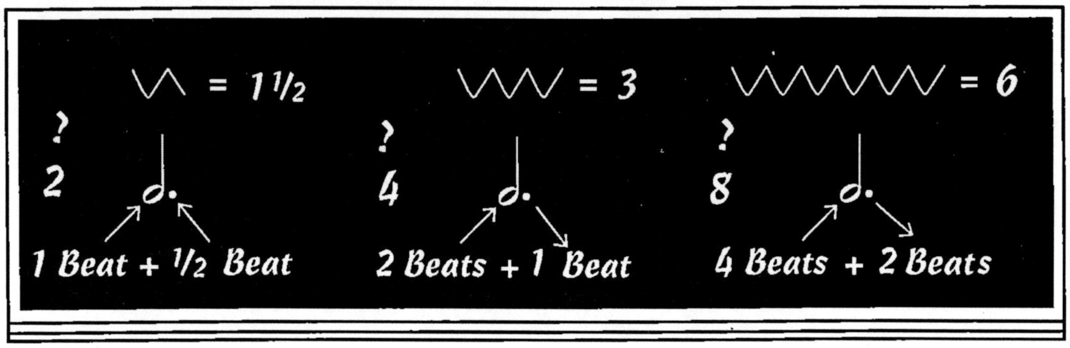

3) Mix 2˙ with all current rhythms, add a time signature, RULES to the left, notate, and have students count/sizzle/sing/play.

4) Student text pgs. 10 & 11. NOTE VALUE CHART #2, pg. 39

1˙/2

1) Sizzle the rhythm and instruct the students to join you when they can. Allow **2 beats** of silence between each repetition. **a)** Explain that the subdivision of 1 is tied to the **down beat** of the subdivision of 2. **b)** Add a time signature, notation and the "tie". Complete the illustration. **Isolate** the dotted quarter note for students to count; pronounced: "wu-un-dot". Students are to **freeze** their foot on the "•"/down of beat 2. Once the students gain confidence add the "&" of beat 2. Make sure the foot **freezes** on the **up beat**. **c)** Explain the number symbol. Illustrate in all GAMES.

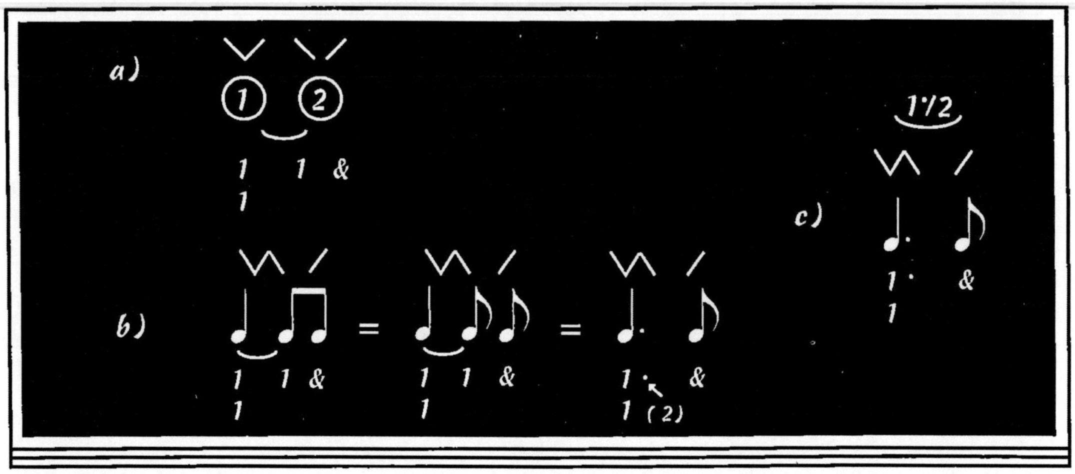

2) Mix 1˙/2 with all current rhythms. Add a time signature, RULES to the left, notate, and have the students count/sizzle/sing/play.

3) Student text pgs. 16 & 17. NOTE VALUE CHART #4, pg. 40.

2/1·

1) Explain and illustrate that the dotted quarter-eighth note can be **reversed** to eighth note-dotted quarter note. Pronounced: "one, and-two-oo" or "bat, m-a-an". Illustrate for all GAMES.

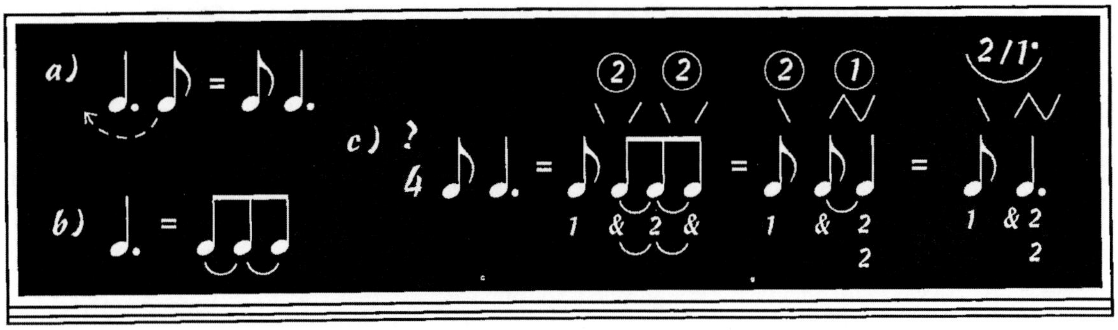

2) Student text pg. 28. NOTE VALUE CHART #4, pg. 40.

1·/4 & 4/1·

1) Explain and illustrate the comparison of 1·/4 to 1·/2. Illustrate for all GAMES.
Pronounced: "wu-un-dot, an-da". Pronounced: "one-e and-two-oo".

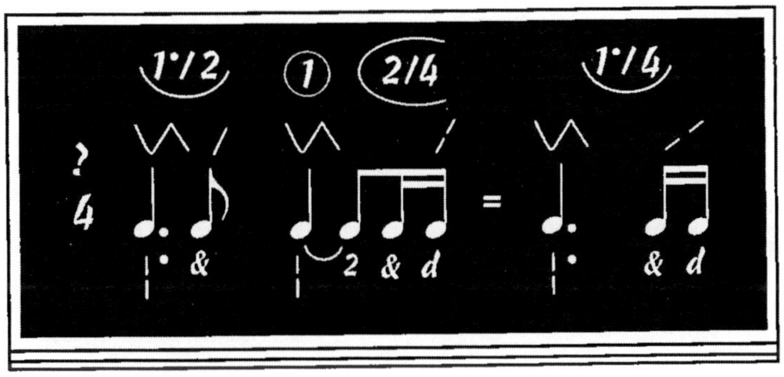

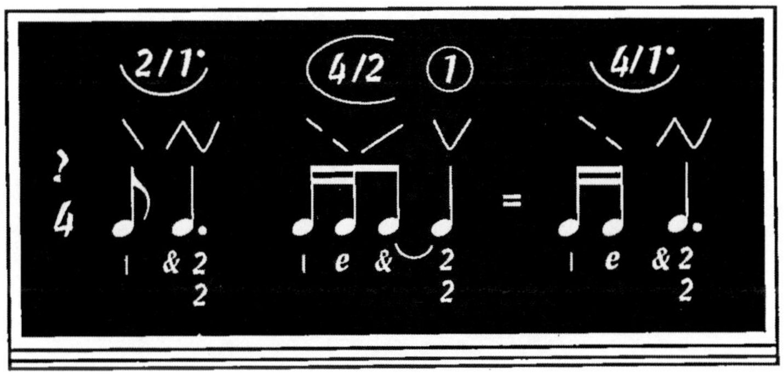

2) Mix 1·/4 with all current rhythms. Add a time signature, RULES to the left, notate, and have the students count/sizzle/sing/play.

3) Student text pg. 28. NOTE VALUE CHART #7, pg. 42.

Review

1) The new rhythmic category is called TIE
2) Definition for TIE rhythms: rhythms that last longer than 1 beat
3) To the main note you TIE subdivisions and/or combinations

Comments

- *If students have a tendency to rush the tempo, reinforce the* ***never in-between****. Remind them that "the mouth follows the foot"*
- *After trying many different syllables for the 1·/2 rhythms, I have found that none compare to "wu-un-dot, and."*
- *Once the 1·/2 rhythm has been internalized, explain the following optical illusions:*

1.  *Most students will associate the* ***first*** *eighth note with the* ***second*** *dotted quarter note.*

2.  *Most students will give the dotted quarter note* ***1 beat*** *and try to play* ***3 eight notes*** *in* ***1 beat****.*

LESSON 11 The Musical Game Board

1) Explain that games like monopoly, checkers and chess require a **game board.** The GAMES OF MUSIC also requires a game board. Explain and illustrate the 5 lines and 4 spaces that make up the musical staff/game board.

MUSICAL STAFF: 5 lines and 4 spaces

2) Explain and illustrate that the lines and spaces represent specific letters of the alphabet. The regular alphabet starts on "A" and ends on "Z". The MUSICAL ALPHABET starts on "C" and ends on "C" (FROM C TO SHINING C). The regular alphabet goes from left to right, whereas the MUSICAL ALPHABET goes up and down **both directions** (you may want to teach the lines and spaces as they learn that specific pitch on their instrument).

3) Explain and illustrate how the clef sign is used to designate the letters for the lines and spaces. Explain ledger ("letter" lines) later.

"G" CLEF

"F" CLEF

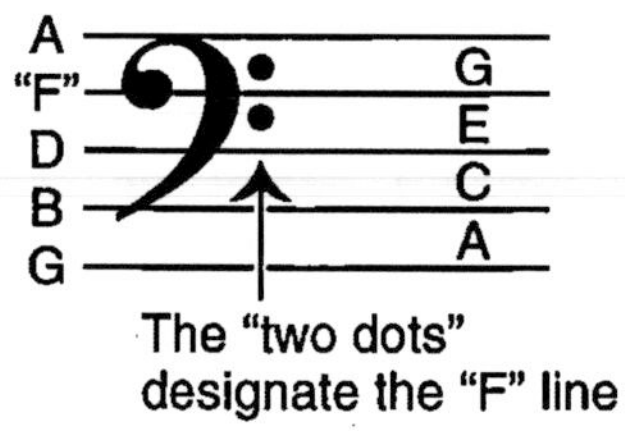

"C" CLEF

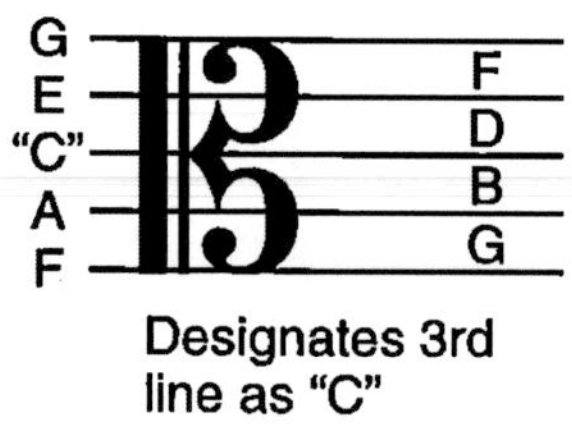

4) **a)** Explain and illustrate the bar line(s) and measure. **b)** Write the following rhythmic sequence **4 times** (one directly below the other). Add a ?/4 to the first line, 2/4 to the second line, 3/4 to the third line, and 4/4 to the fourth line. **Place** bar lines accordingly. Explain that neither the **top number** of the time signature or the placement of the **bar lines** has anything to do with how you count the **basic** rhythm.

a)

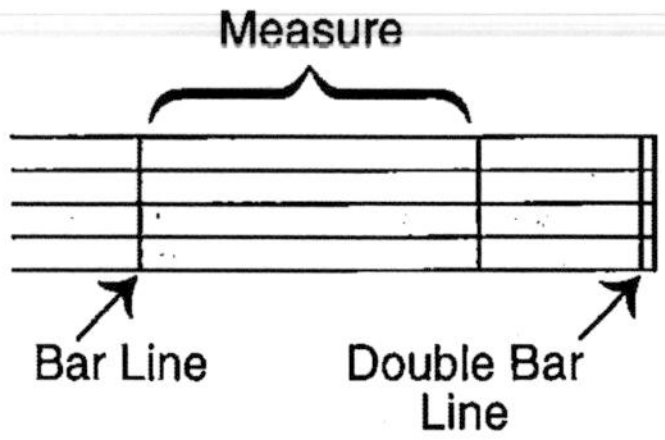

b)

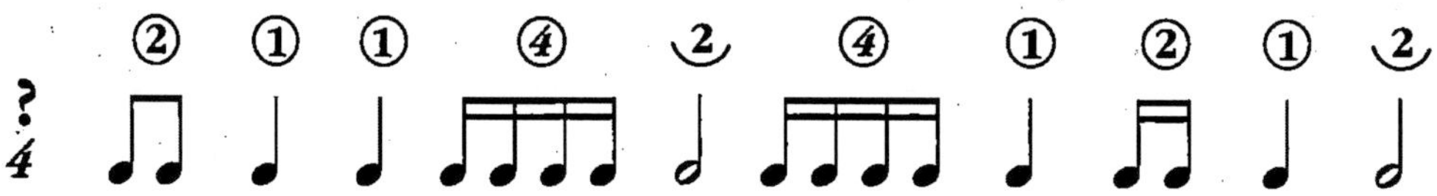

NOTICE: Continue to use "1" for **each beat** of the measure until ①, ②, ④, 2, 2', and 4 have been internalized! Near the end of the first semester or the beginning of the second semester, instruct the students to change the "1" 's to the appropriate numbers within the measure.

LESSON 12 Sight Reading

Objectives

- Transfer "mental" rhythms to "physical performance"
- Transfer "mental" pitches to "physical performance"
- Transfer "mental" rhythms and pitches at a sight reading level

Procedure

Ones success in sight-reading begins with rhythmic feel, association, recognition and internalization. However, there is another area that needs to be developed before one can be successful in the art of sight-reading. After rhythmic recognition comes **RHYTHMIC** and **PITCH TRANSFER**. When one fails to sight-read, it does not necessarily mean that one "can't count". The problem is due to the inability of the student to quickly transfer what he or she sees on the written sheet of music to the actual playing of that melodic line on their instrument.

The following exercises are to help the students **TRANSFER** what they see on paper to their instrument. The ability to do this transfer **quickly** is the key to sight-reading.

SIGHT-READING is a "doing" phenomenon; the more one sight-reads the better they become. However, sight-reading skills deteriorate if one stops sight-reading or does not sight-read often. This sight-reading skill tends to diminish faster than other skills that have been mastered.

Rhythmic/Pitch Transfer

EXERCISE #1: Using **current** pitches, say one pitch at a time and instruct the students to play it on their instrument as fast as possible. Make sure they hold it long enough to insure characteristic tones. Turn this into a game by selecting 2 students. The one that plays the pitch first, wins.

EXERCISE #2: Draw a musical staff, add a clef and instruct the students to say the pitch of the line or space **you point** to. Turn this into a game as well.

EXERCISE #3: Draw a musical staff, add a clef and place **different** notes on **current** lines and spaces. Point to the various notes and instruct them to play the correct pitch on their instrument. The notes **do not** represent the **length** of sound at this time. Also use as a game.

EXERCISE #4: GAME. Draw 2 musical staffs. Select 2 students and instruct them to place an "x" on the **line** or space that correctly **represents** the **pitch** that you give them. The first one to place the "x" wins.

EXERCISE #5: Using **current pitches** and rhythms, write various rhythms on a staff. Keep the pitches the **same** for each particular rhythm. Select a **slow** tempo with the metronome and instruct the students to play the rhythm when you point to it. You can make this more demanding by increasing the tempo.

EXERCISE #6: Same as exercise #5, except use **2 different pitches** per exercise.

EXERCISE #7: Same as exercise #6, except use **more than 1 pitch** per rhythm. Keep increasing the amount of information per measure until key signatures, accidentals, ties, slurs, etc. are accomplished.

LESSON 13 Rests-Silent Sound

Objectives

- **Definition for rest**
- **Recognition of rests through number symbols and notation**

Warm Up

1) **Count/sizzle/sing/play basic rhythms with sign language.**
2) **Count/sizzle/sing/play a rhythmic sequence from the board.**
3) **Notate the sequence, erase the number symbols, then count/sizzle/sing/play.**
4) **Student text.**

Procedure

OVERALL APPROACH TO RESTS: Rests will basically be treated like their corresponding note. The differences are:

- "( )" are placed around the counting syllables
- Foot/note symbols are "hollowed" ex. V = V (hollowed)
- "**Whisper**" the counting syllables
- "R" or "r" are used in the number symbols

NOTE: When students count **the number symbols for rest's**, they are to whisper during the "R's". Example: (R) Students would whisper "wu-un". R2 Students whisper "wu-un-two-oo" , etc.

1) **a)** Explain and illustrate that **every note** has a **corresponding rest** of **equal** value/length. Explain that the the "musical mirror" reflects the **stems** and **flags** only. Like most mirrors, the reflection is backwards. The quarter, half, and whole notes are reflected in a circus mirror which explains the distortion. **b)** The WHOLE HANGS from the 4th line and the HALF SITS on the 3rd line. **Both rests** are located on the 3rd space.

2) Explain and illustrate that (R) is the corresponding number symbol for (1). Place several (R)'s on the board for students to whisper. Next, mix several (R)'s and (1)'s for students to count. Finally, mix (R) with all current rhythms. After the number symbols have been internalized, notate in all GAMES. Do not teach R2 and R4 until (R) has been internalized.

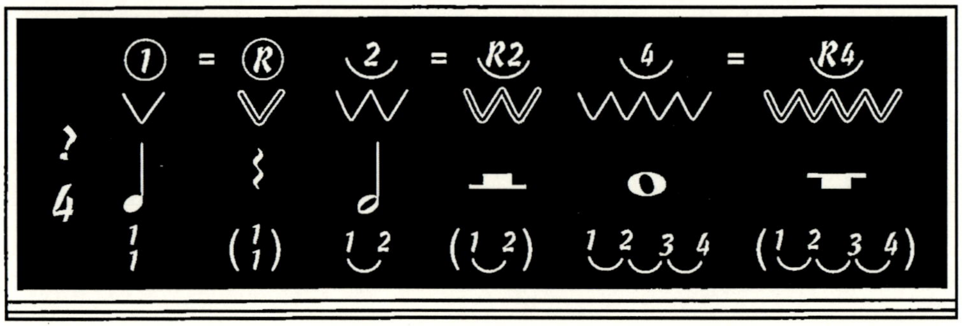

3) Mix the new rhythm with all current rhythms. Add a time signature, RULES to the left, notate and have students count/sizzle/sing/play.

4) Student text pgs. 12 & 13. NOTE VALUE CHART #3, pg. 40.

2/r r/2 r/4 4/r

1) Explain and illustrate the following comparisons. Do not teach all rhythms at one time. Remember, have the students imitate your sizzle first, then explain the sign language, next explain the number symbols, and finally notate in all GAMES.

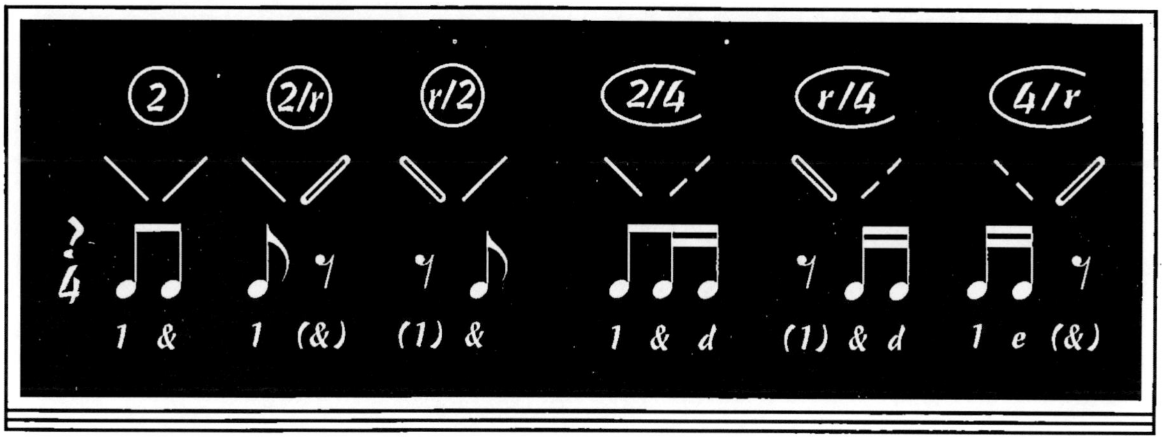

2) Mix each new rhythm with all current rhythms. Add a time signature, RULES to the left, notate and have the students count/sizzle/sing/play.

3) (r/2) & (2/r) located on student text pgs. 14 & 15. NOTE VALUE CHART #3, pg. 40.

4) (4/r) & (r/4) located on student text pg. 29. NOTE VALUE CHART #5, pg.41.

Rests Associated With (3)

1) **a)** Explain and illustrate the following comparisons. **b)** The notation for GAME 4 looks the same as FAST GAME 8, however a "3" will usually appear above or below the rhythm. Do not teach all new rhythms at one time.

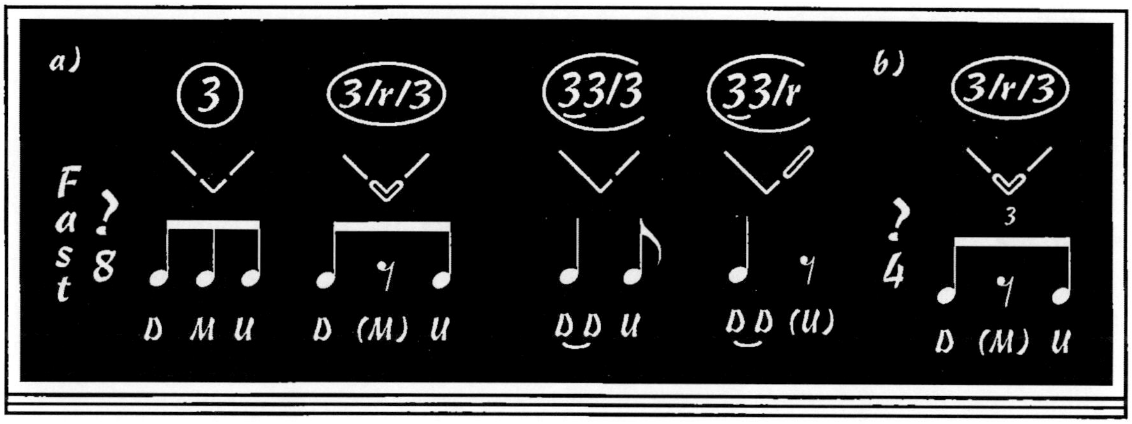

2) Mix each new rhythm with all current rhythms. Add a time signature, RULES to the left, notate and have the students count/sizzle/sing/play.

3) Student text pgs. 34, & 35. NOTE VALUE CHART #9, pg. 42 & #10 pg. 43.

Rests Associated With (6)

1) **a)** Explain and illustrate the following comparisons. Keep reminding the students that the **basic feel** is that of a (3). **b)** The notation for GAME 4 looks the **same** as FAST GAME 8, however a "6" will usually appear above or below the rhythm.

2) Mix each new rhythm with all current rhythms. Add a time signature, RULES to the left, notate and have the students count/sizzle/sing/play.

3) NOTE VALUE CHART #12, pg. 43.

Review

1) **Rest = Silent Sound**
2) **Recognition of all rests through sign language, number symbols and notation**

Comments

- *Explain that a whole rests can also mean the **"whole" measure** is silent, **regardless** of the **number** of **beats** indicated by the time signature.*
- *Whenever there is a breakdown in playing or sight-reading, one must decide if the problem is due to **knowledge** or the **transfer** of knowledge to their instrument. Many times a student will say they **do not** understand a rhythm when they actually do. Have them start with the bottom number of the time signature, the RULES,etc., and they will end up giving you all of the correct answers for the rhythm.*
- *Remember, if you are not achieving the desired results, chances are, you are going too **fast. Fast** could mean **tempo or subject matter.***
- *When needed, explain the following optical illusions:*

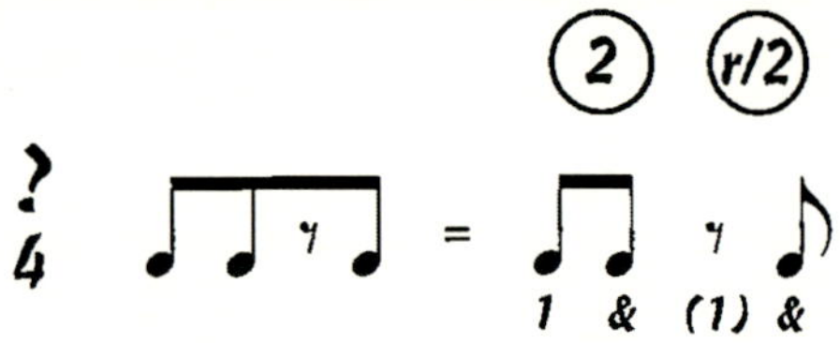

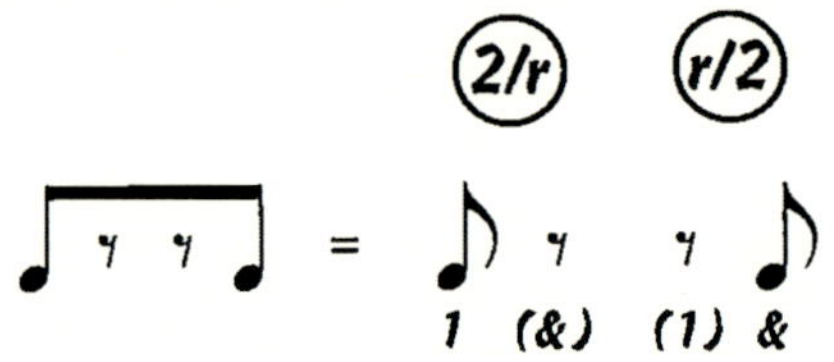

The eighth note belongs to the eighth rest, not the quarter note. Most students will give the eighth rest 1 beat and play the eighth note on beat 2.

- *Remind the students that when you change the time signature it **does not** change the rhythms. It just changes the notes that **represent** the rhythms.*

LESSON 14 Combination Rhythms

Objectives

- Definition for COMBINATION rhythms
- Recognition of COMBINATIONS through sign language, number symbols, notation

Warm Up

1) **Count/sizzle/sing/play basic rhythms with sign language.**
2) **Count/sizzle/sing/play a rhythmic sequence from the board.**
3) **Notate the sequence, erase the number symbols, then count/sizzle/sing/play.**
4) **Student text.**

Procedure

1) Direct, tap your foot, sizzle (2/4) and instruct the students to join you when they can. Next, explain the sign language.

2) **a)** You can relate this concept to pizza. **b)** Explain that mushroom represents the (2) and pepperoni represents the (4). Illustrate that you took the down beat from the (2) and the up beat from the (4). **c)** The " C " stands for combination and the "/" stands for 1/2 of the (2) and 1/2 of the (4), **NOT** 2 notes or 4 notes. Add the definition and emphasize that COMBINATION is a new category of rhythm .

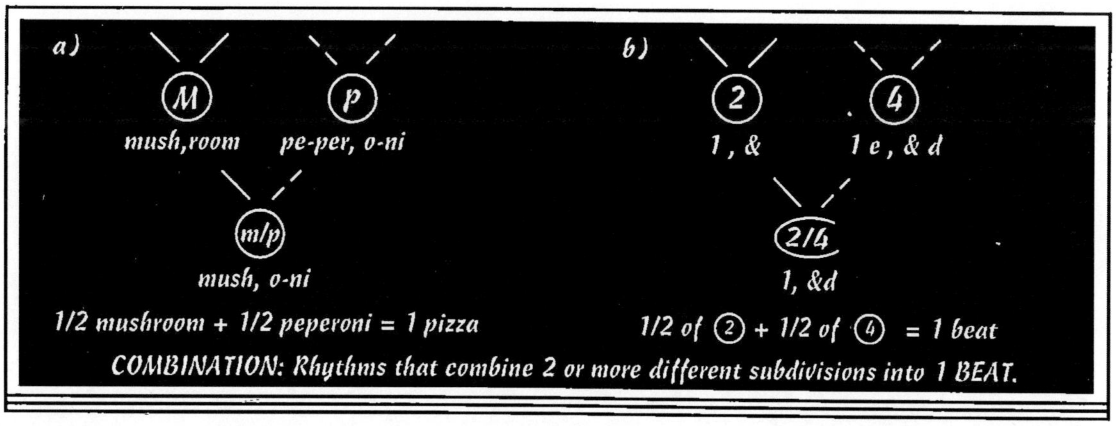

3) Have students count/sizzle several (2/4)'s using sign language. Next, mix with all rhythms.
4) Write several (2/4)'s on the board for students to count/sizzle. Next, mix with all rhythms.
5) Explain and illustrate the notation for (2/4). Illustrate in all GAMES.

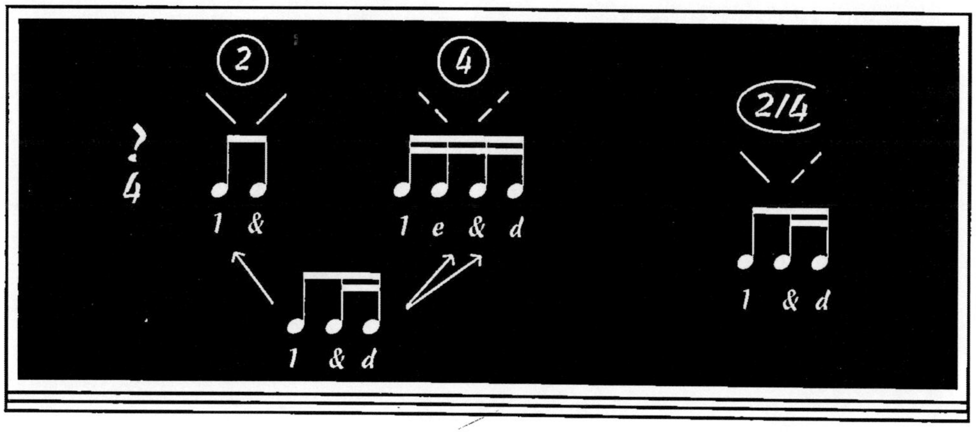

6) Mix (2/4) with all current rhythms. Add a time signature, RULES to the left, notate and have the students count/sizzle/sing/play.

7) Student text pgs. 20 & 21. NOTE VALUE CHART #5, pg. 41.

8) Use the same procedure to explain and illustrate (4/2) (pe-per, room). Illustrate for all GAMES.

9) Student text pgs. 20 & 21. NOTE VALUE CHART #5, pg. 41.

Combinations for ③

WHEN A COUNTING SYLLABLE IS TIED TO ANOTHER SYLLABLE, THE **SECOND** SYLLABLE BECOMES A **PULSATION** OF THE **FIRST** SYLLABLE:

DD - pulsate the word "down" to sound like "dow-own"

MM - pulsate the word "mid" to sound like "mi-id"

UU - pulsate the word "up" to sound like "u-up"

1) **a)** Explain and illustrate that you **tie** the **first** 2 eighth notes of a ③ to form (33/3). Alternate between"down-mid-up" and "dow-own-up". **Point** to the counting syllables as they count. **b)** After (33/3) is internalized, use the same procedure for (3/33). **c)** Explain the notation for (3/33) in GAME 4.

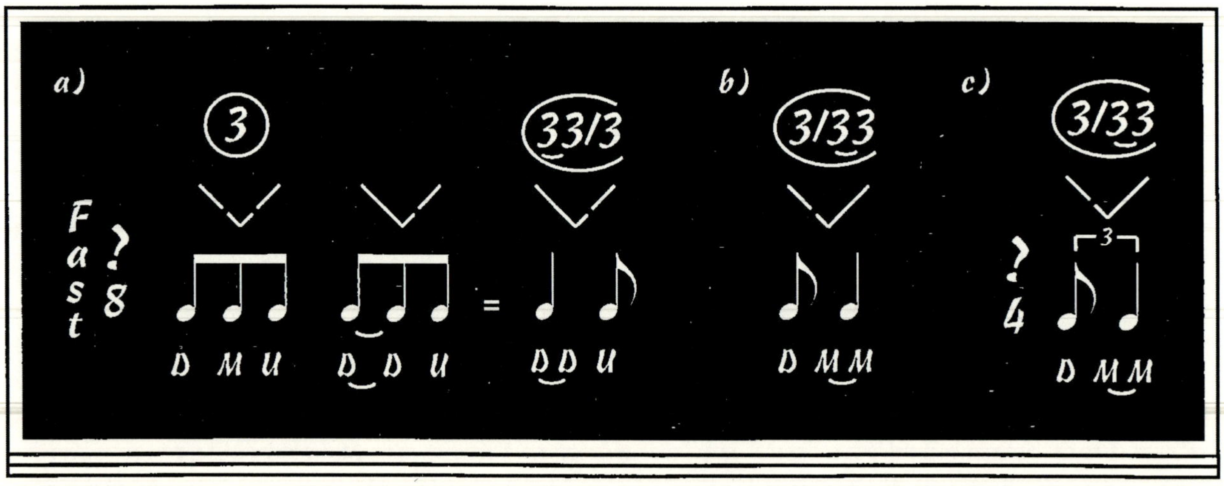

2) Mix (33/3) with ③. Add a time signature, RULES to the left, notate, and have the students count/sizzle/sing/play. Once internalized, mix with all current rhythms.

3) Student text pgs. 32 & 33. NOTE VALUE CHART #9, pg. 42.

Combination for ⑥

1) **a)** Explain and illustrate that the COMBINATIONS for ⑥ are formed by **dividing** the eighth notes of a ③. **b)** Explain the notation for the (2/6) rhythm in GAME 4.

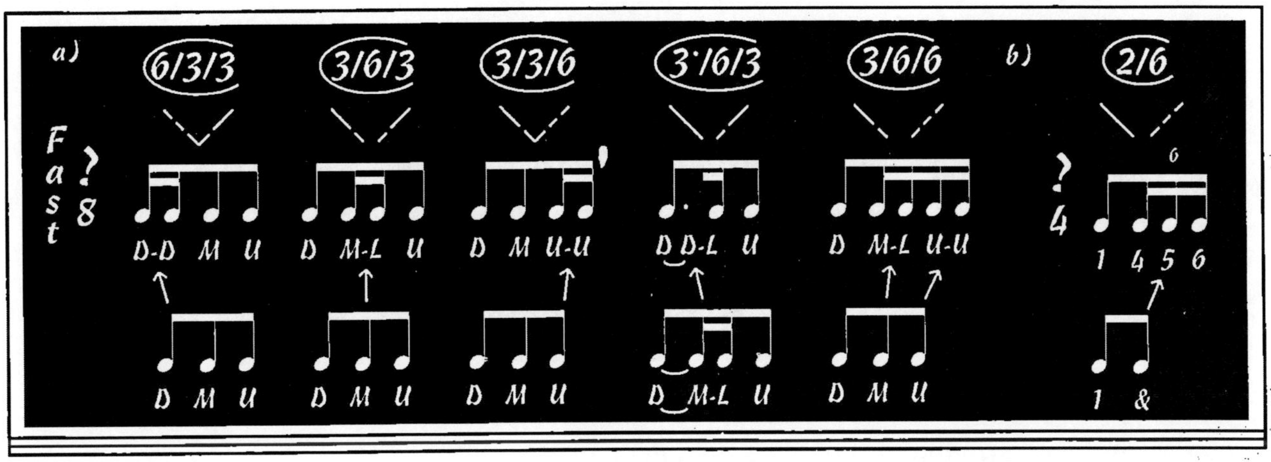

2) Mix each new rhythm with all current rhythms. Add a time signature, RULES to the left, notate and have the students count/sizzle/sing/play.

3) Student text pgs. 36 & 37. NOTE VALUE CHART #11, pg. 43. GAMES 2 & 4 CHART #6, pg. 41.
4) Explain the relationship of FAST GAME 8 to GAME 4.

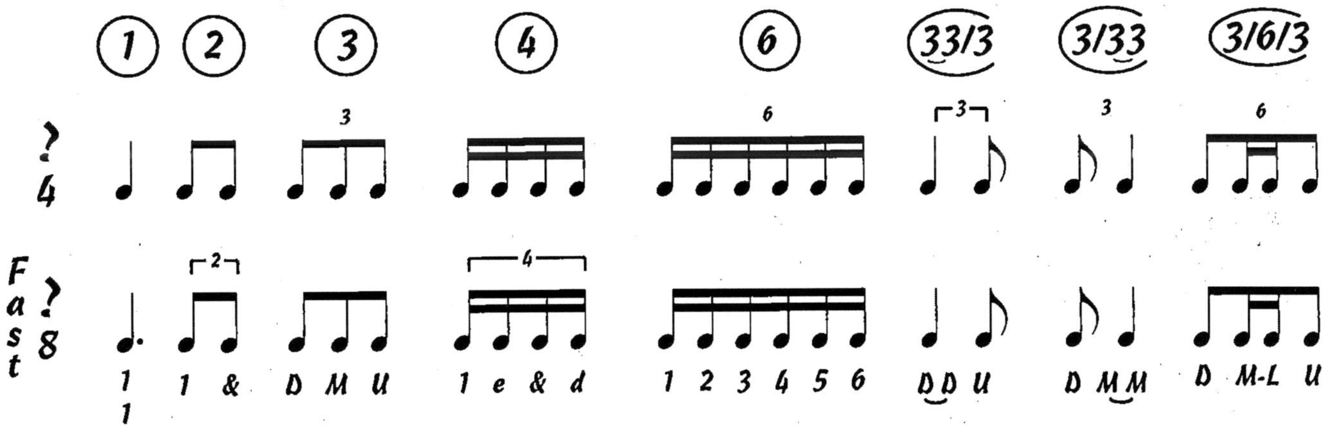

Review

1) The new rhythmic category is called COMBINATION
2) Definition for combination rhythms: combine 2 or more different subdivisions within 1 beat
3) Demonstrate the sign language
4) The "C" in the number symbol stands for COMBINATION
5) In FAST GAME 8 the ③ is the rhythm that all others are based upon

LESSON 15 Syncopation

Objectives

- Definition for SYNCOPATION
- Recognition of SYNCOPATION through number symbols and notation

Warm Up

1) **Count/sizzle/sing/play basic rhythms with sign language.**
2) **Count/sizzle/sing/play a rhythmic sequence from the board.**
3) **Notate the sequence, erase the number symbols, then count/sizzle/sing/play.**
4) **Student text.**

Procedure

1) Direct, tap your foot, sizzle a syncopated pattern (ex. 4/4 eighth, quarter, eighth) and instruct the students to join you when they can. Allow **1 beat of silence** between each repetition.

2) Explain and illustrate that you take a ② and **divide** it with a ①. Explain that "∧" is the **same length** of time as "∨"; it starts on the **up beat** rather than the down beat. Syncopation is pronounced "one, and-two, and". Instruct the students to **accent and connect** the "and-two". Notate in all GAMES.

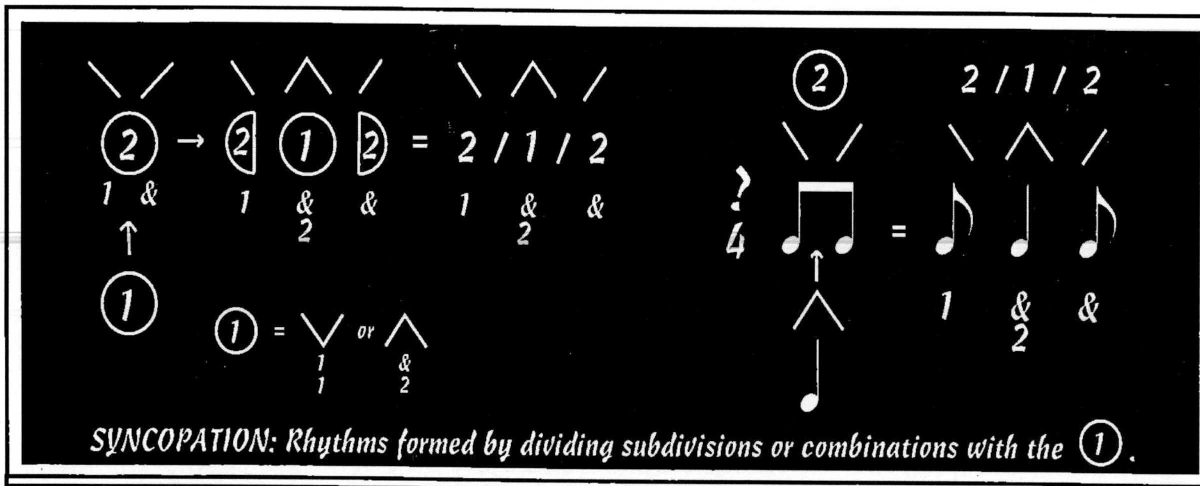

3) Mix 2/1/2 with all current rhythms. Add a time signature, RULES to the left, notate and have the students count/sizzle/sing/play.

4) Student text pgs. 18 & 19. NOTE VALUE CHART #4, pg. 40.

5) Use the same procedure to explain and illustrate 4/1/4, 2/1/4 and 4/1/2.

6) Student text pgs. 18 & 19. NOTE VALUE CHART #4, pg. 40.

7) Explain and illustrate that rests can be substituted for the first or last part of a syncopated rhythm. Illustrate for all GAMES.

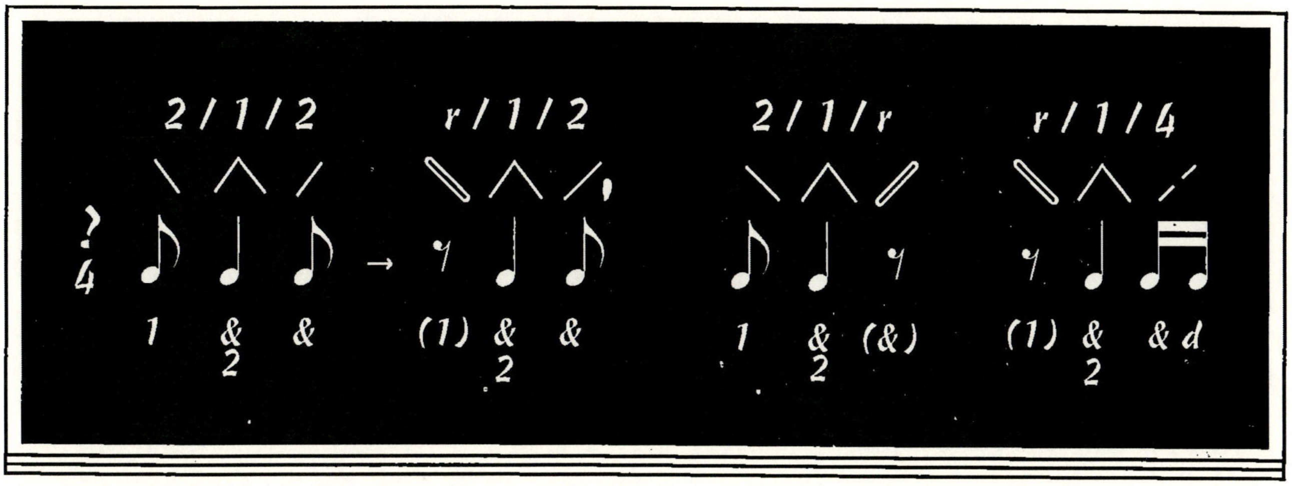

8) Student text pg. 29.

9) When **appropriate,** explain and illustrate that you can syncopate subdivisions and combinations **more** than 1 time. All you do is **add more** (1)'s in the middle of the rhythm.

1/1/1

1) Explain and illustrate that "1" in the **number symbol** stands for the (1) (the main note of the GAME). **Normally** the main note receives 1 beat. **However,** we now have to **perform** 3 of them in **2 beats!** Select GAME 4 and explain that you **substituted** 2 eighth notes for each quarter note. You can now **divide 6** notes by **2** beats equally. Inform the students that when they say the letter "**p**" of "dow-own, u-up", their foot should be on the **down** of **beat 2** . Have the students practice this portion of the rhythm several times. Next, add the "mi-id". Finally have the students alternate between "down-mid-up,down-mid-up" and "dow-own, u-up, mi-id".

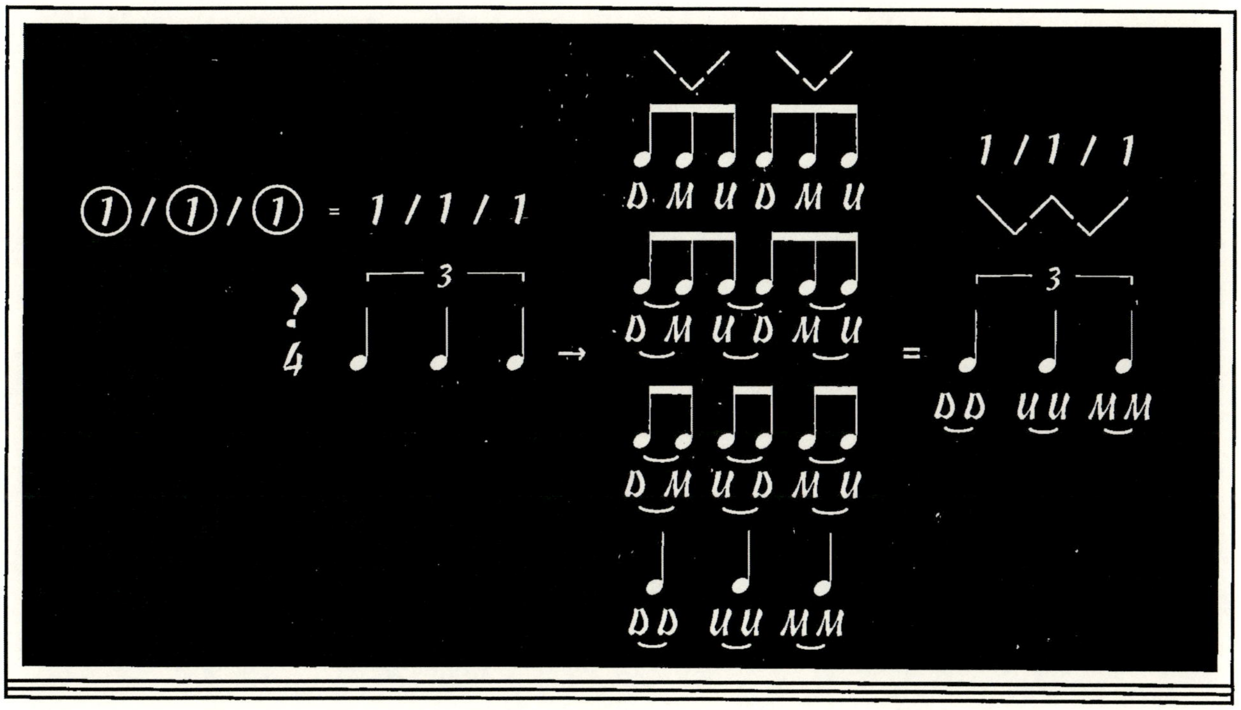

2) Have the students repeat the following sequence several times. They are to count/sizzle/sing and play:

||: (3) (3) 1/1/1 :||

3) Student text pg. 38. NOTE VALUE CHART #6, pg. 41.

Review

1) **The new rhythm is called SYNCOPATION**
2) **Syncopation requires at least 2 beats**
3) **The number symbol is 2/1/2**
4) **Definition for syncopation: rhythms that are formed by dividing subdivisions or combinations with the (1)/time signature note**

Comments

- *Explain that syncopation is one of the* ***4 categories*** *for all rhythms.*
- *Do not teach all forms of syncopation at one time. However, teach 2/1/2 & 4/1/4 at the* ***same*** *time.* ***Afterwards****, explain that they will see 2/1/2 the most.*
- *When needed, explain the following optical illusion:*

LESSON 16 The "W" Sisters

Objectives

- Recognition of (w·/d), (w/ē/d), & (w/e) through number symbols and notation
- Counting syllables

Warm Up

1) Count/sizzle/sing/play basic rhythms with sign language.
2) Count/sizzle/sing/play a rhythmic sequence from the board.
3) Notate the sequence, erase the number symbols, then count/sizzle/sing/play.
4) Student text.

Procedure

1) Direct, tap your foot, sizzle (w·/d) and instruct the students to join you when they can. Allow **1 beat** of silence between each repetition.

2) **a)** Explain and illustrate that the "parents" of the "W" sisters are Mr. and Mrs. (4). **b)** To **find** the **first** sister you **tie** the **first 3** notes together. The "e" and the "&" become a **pulsation** of the "1": 1͜1͜1 = "wu-u-un". You can add that she is **nervous**. The "d" is pronounced as usual. **c)** When you count the rhythm out loud it sounds like the name Wanda. Alternate between a (4) and (w·/d); pronounced: "wu-u-un da". Explain the number symbol. **Note:** If you do not use "1-e-&-d" for (4), use (2·/4) for the number symbol. **d)** Notate in all GAMES.

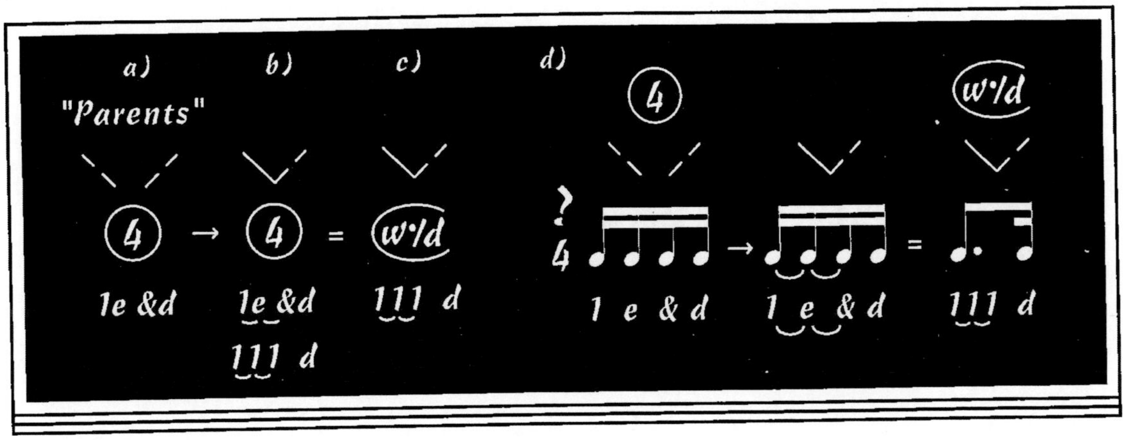

3) Write a rhythmic sequence using (4) and (w·/d) for students to count/sizzle.

4) Mix (w·/d) with all current rhythms. Add a time signature RULES to the left, notate and have the students count/sizzle/sing/play.

5) Student text pgs. 22, 23 and 27. Use page 26 if you use syllables other than "1-e-&-d". NOTE VALUE CHART # 5, pg. 41.

w/ē/d & w/e·

1) Use the same procedure to explain and illustrate w/ē/d or 4/2/4 and w/e· or 4/2·.
   - Students **imitate** your sizzle
   - Explain **which notes** of the "parents" are tied
   - Explain the number symbol
   - Notate in all GAMES
   - **Alternate** between (4) and the "sister" (verbally, then with number symbols).
   - Mix with all current rhythms

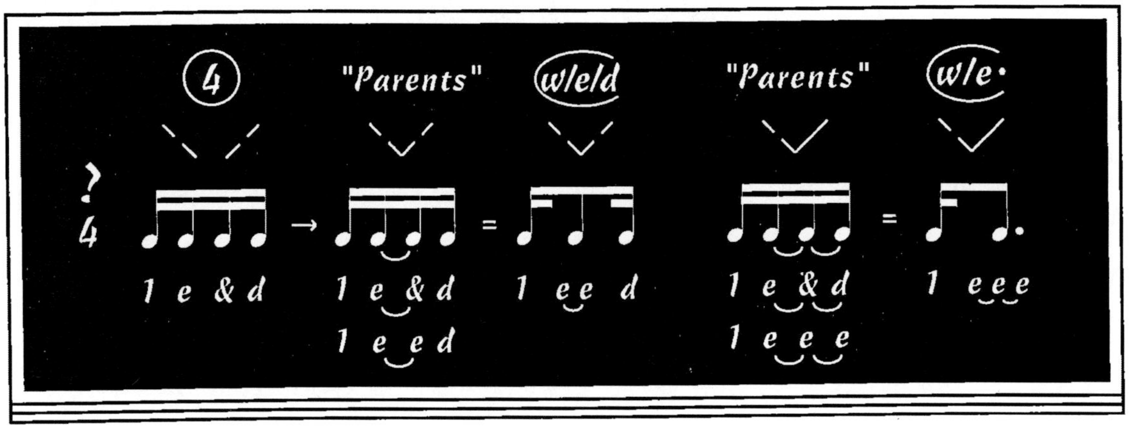

2) Student text pgs. 24, 25 & 27. NOTE VALUE CHART # 5, pg. 41.
3) When needed, relate 4·8/4·8 to a (8). Explain that you tie the first 3 notes of the **down** beat and the first 3 notes of the **up** beat. At first, pronounce: "wu-u-un da" on the down beat and the up beat. Once internalized it is to be pronounced "wu-u-un da, a-a-an da". Student text pg. 29 & CHART #8, pg. 42.

Review

1) The parents of the "W" sisters are the (4)'s
2) Tie the first 3 notes for w·/d or 2·/4
3) Tie the middle 2 notes for w/ē/d or 4/2/4
4) Tie the last 3 notes for w/e· or 4/2·

Comments

- *Teach* w·/d *and* w/ē/d *at the* ***same time.***
- *Explain and illustrate the following when needed:*

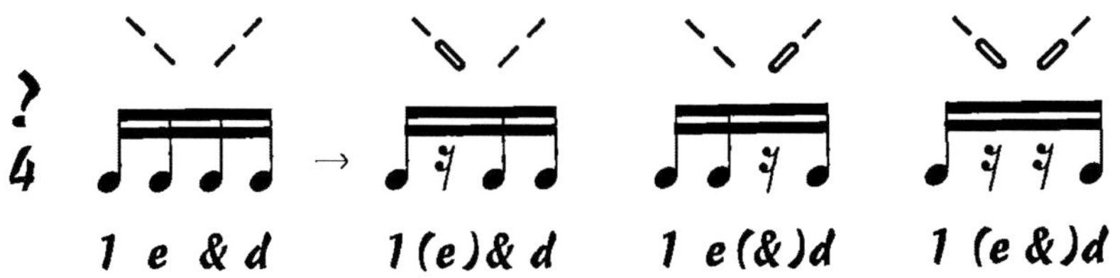

- *Once* w·/d *has been internalized,* ***substitute the numbers*** *within the* ***measure*** *for* 1 1 1.

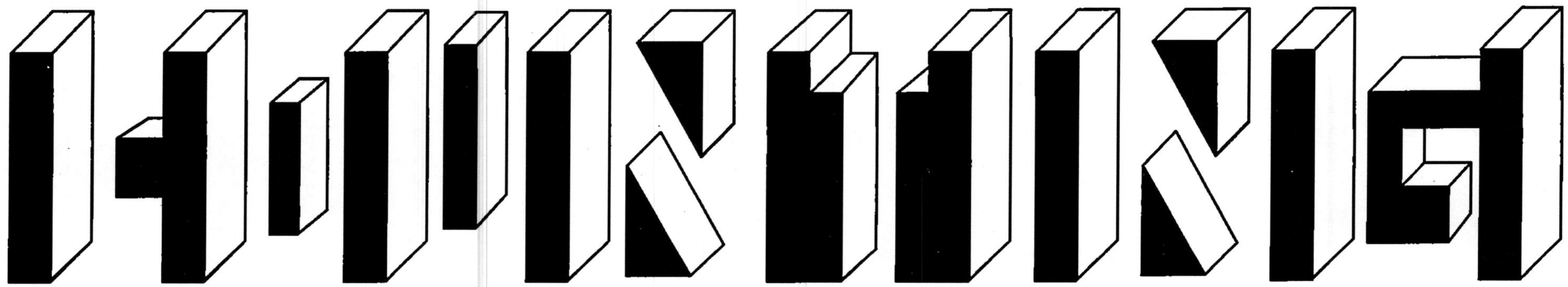

IS AN OPTICAL ILLUSION

Note Values

(5 minute test)

____________________ (Name)

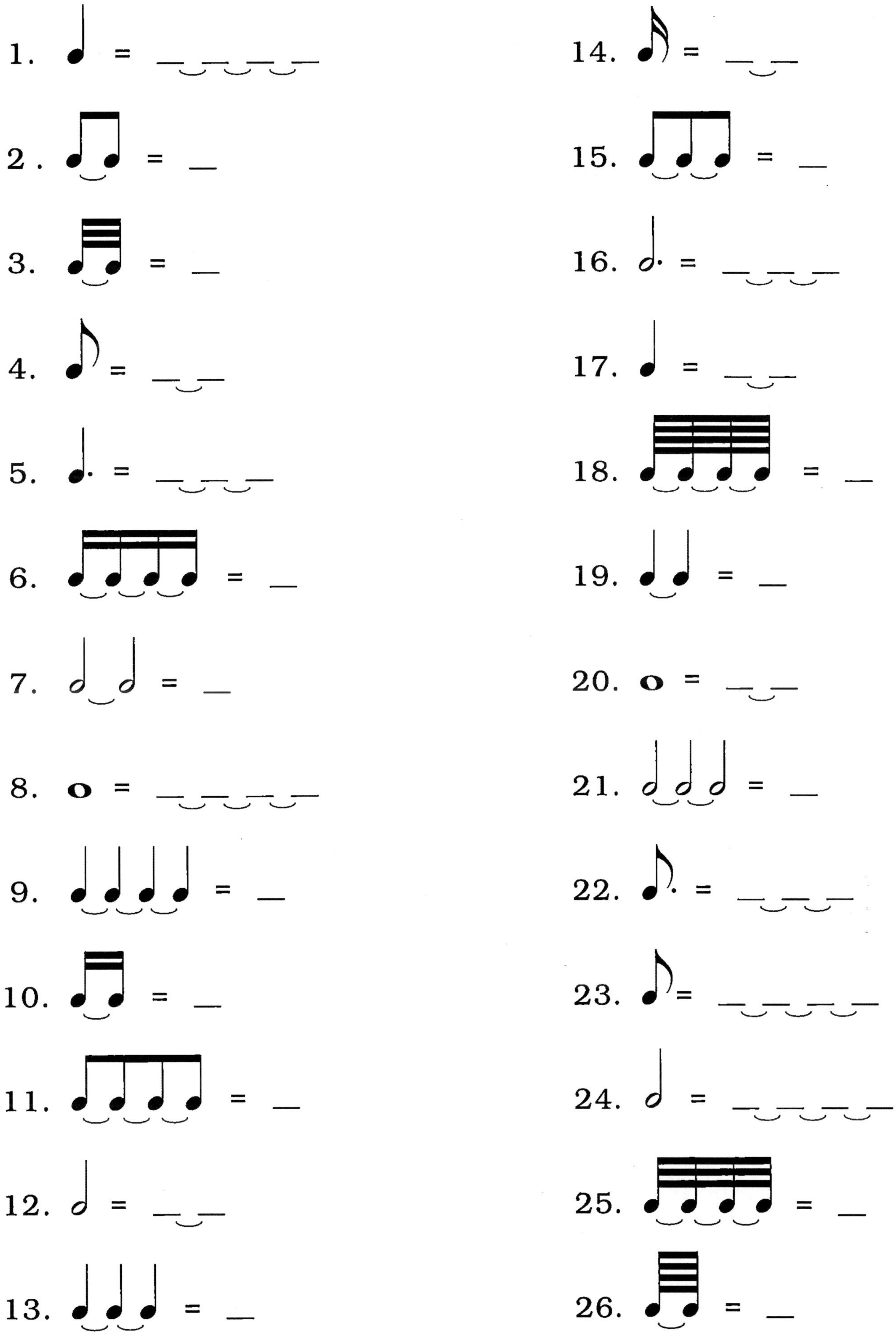

THE GAMES OF MUSIC

______________________ (Name)

1. Counting is an ______________ ______________.

2. What are the 3 qualities of a successful counter ?

   A. ______________

   B. ______________

   C. ______________

3. What are the 3 functions of the foot ?

   A. ______________

   B. ______________

   C. ______________

4. What is the definition for SUBDIVISION ? ______________

5. Definition for (4). ______________

6. Definition for (2). ______________

7. Definition for (1). ______________

8. Draw and name the musical notes.

   o ______________ *o* ______________ *o* ______________

   o ______________ *o* ______________ *o* ______________ *o* ______________

9. Time signatures stand for the ______________

10. What are the 3 "purposes" of the bottom number of the time signature?

    A. ______________

    B. ______________

    C. ______________

11. How do you find the (1) ? ______________

12. How do you find the (2) ? ______________

13. How do you find the (4) ? ______________

______________________________ (Name)

14. Fill in the correct note values.

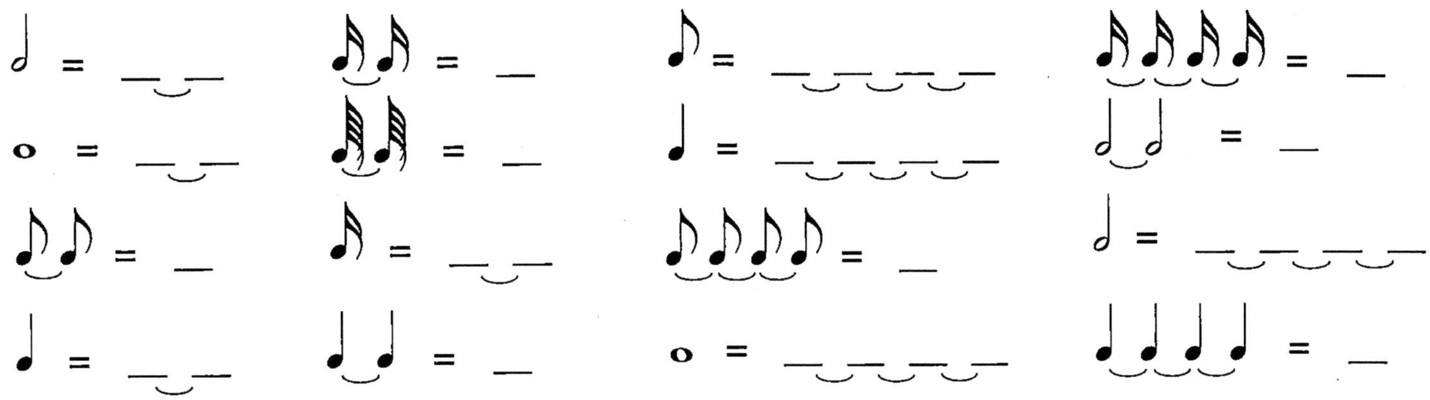

15. Complete the notation for the following GAMES.

	GAME	1	2	4
Foot				
16				
Count				
4				
1				

16. Write the notes that represent the following rhythmic sequence. Write the foot symbols above each note and the counting syllables below each note.

(1) (4) (1) (2) (4) (2) (1)

4

17. Write the definition for TIE rules. ______________________________

18. What notes do you tie together for tie rules? ______________________________

19. What are the 3 rules of a dot ?

A. ______________________________

B. ______________________________

C. ______________________________

____

(Name)

20. Complete the notation for the following GAMES.

	①	②	2	④	4	2·
Foot						
♩/4						
Count						
♩/2						
♩/8						

21. Write the notes that represent the following rhythmic sequence. Write the foot symbols above each note and the counting syllables below each note.

① 2 ② 2 4 ④ ② 2·

♩/8

22. Write the number symbols and foot symbols above each note for the following rhythmic sequence. Write the counting syllables below each note.

♩/4 

23. What is the definition for RESTS ? ______________________________

24. Draw the appropriate rest for each note.

(Name)

25. Complete the notation for the following GAMES.

	(1)	2	(R)	R4	4	R2
Foot ? 4 Count						
? 2						
? 8						

26. Write the notes/rests that represent the following rhythmic sequence. Write the foot symbols above each note/rest and the counting syllables below each note/rest.

(4) 2• (1) (R) R4 (2) R2 2 4

?
2

27. Write the number symbols and foot symbols above each note/rest for the following rhythmic sequence. Write the counting syllables below each note/rest.

28. Write the MUSICAL ALPHABET.

29. Write the definition for a MUSICAL STAFF.

____
(Name)

30. 𝄞 or 𝄢 or 𝄡 is called a ______________________ ______________

31. Draw a musical staff, add a clef sign and a time signature in the proper order.

32. What are the following ?

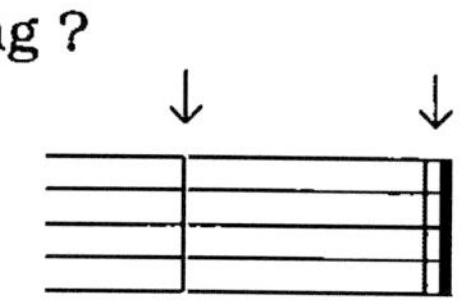

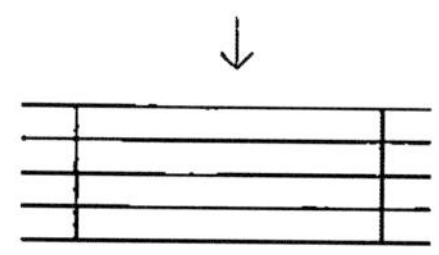

______________________ & ______________________ ______________________

33. What does the TOP NUMBER of the time signature tell you ?

____

34. Place bar lines where needed.

35. What pitches do the following " ■ " indicate. Circle the clef for your instrument.

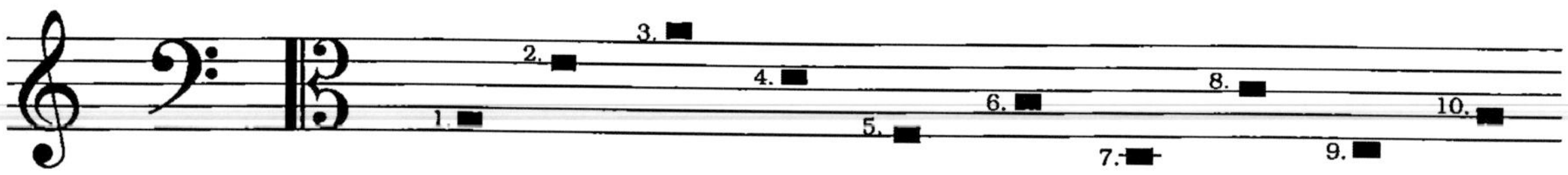

1. ______________________
2. ______________________
3. ______________________
4. ______________________
5. ______________________
6. ______________________
7. ______________________
8. ______________________
9. ______________________
10. ______________________

(Name) ______________________

36. Complete the notation for the following GAMES.

	(1)	(r/2)	(R)	(2/r)	4	(2)
Foot						
4						
Count						
2						
8						

37. Write the notes/rests that represent the following rhythmic sequence. Write the foot symbols above each note/rest and the counting syllables below each note/rest.

(4) 2• (1) (r/2) R4 (2) 2 (R) (2/r) (1)

8

38. Complete the notation for the following GAMES.

	(2)	2	(1)	R4	1·/2	R2
Foot						
4						
Count						
2						
8						

____
(Name)

39. Write the notes/rests that represent the following rhythmic sequence. Write the foot symbols above each note/rest and the counting syllables below each note/rest.

(4) 1'/2 (1) (r/2) 1'/2 (2) 2 (R) (2/r)

♩ 8

40. Write the definition for COMBINATION rhythms. _______________________________

____

41. Complete the notation for the following GAMES.

	2/4	(r/2)	(R)	(4)	4/2	(2)
Foot						
♩ 4						
Count						
♩ 2						
♩ 8						

42. Write the number symbols and foot symbols above each note/rest for the following rhythmic sequence. Write the counting syllables below each note/rest.

____

(Name)

43. Write the definition for SYNCOPATION . ____

____

44. Complete the notation for the following GAMES.

	2/4	r/2	1	1'/2	2/1/2	2
Foot						
4						
Count						
2						
8						

45. Write the number symbols and foot symbols above each note/rest for the following rhythmic sequence. Write the counting syllables below each note/rest.

46. Write the notes/rests that represent the following rhythmic sequence. Write the foot symbols above each note and the counting syllables below each note/rest. Place bar lines where needed.

1 1'/2 r/2 2/1/2 2 2 R2 4/2

4
8

(Name) ____________________

47. What are the 4 categories for all rhythms ?

1. ____________________

2. ____________________

3. ____________________

4. ____________________

48. Who are the parents of the " W " sisters ? ____________________

49. Complete the notation for the following GAMES.

	2/1/2	(1)	(w·/d)	(r/2)	(w/ē/d)	(w/e·)
Foot						
?/4						
Count						
?/2						
?/8						

50. Write the number symbols and foot symbols above each note/rest for the following rhythmic sequences. Write the counting syllables below each note/rest.

51.

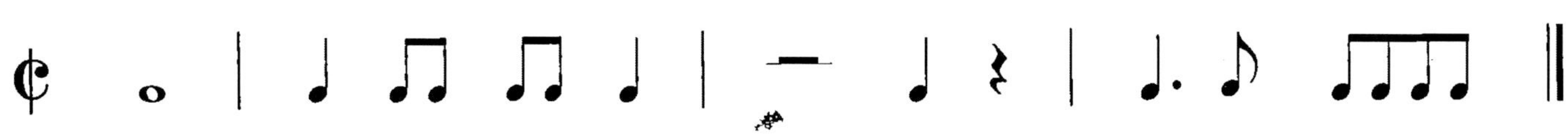

(Name)

52. The notes that represent a (3) look like the notes in a ( ) .

53. Complete the notation for the following GAMES.

	2/1/2	(1)	(3)	(r/2)	(w·/d)	(w/e·)
Foot						
? 4						
Count						
? 2						

54. Write the number symbols and foot symbols above each note/rest for the following rhythmic sequences. Write the counting syllables below each note/rest.

55. In FAST 6/8 , what is the most important SUBDIVISION ? ____________

56. In FAST 6/8 , what note does the bottom number stand for ? __________

57. Complete the notation for Fast 6/8.

	(3)	(1)	(R)	(33/3)	2	(3/33)
Foot						
Fast 6 8						
Count						

59. Write the number symbols and foot symbols above each note/rest for the following rhythmic sequence. Write the counting syllables below each note/rest.

59. Complete the notation for the following GAMES.

	2/1/4	(3)	1/1/1	(r/4)	1·/4	(4/r)
Foot						
› 4						
Count						
› 2						
› 8						

60. Write the notes/rests that represent the following rhythmic sequence. Write the foot symbols above each note/rest and the counting syllables below each note/rest. Add bar lines where needed.

4/1/2 (1) (3) (r/4) (r/2) (w·/d) (R) 1/1/1

5/4

61. The notes that represent a (6) look like the notes in a ( ).

62. Complete the notation for Fast 6/8.

	(6)	(3·/6)	(3·/6/3)	(33/r)	(6/r/3)	(6/6/3)
Foot						
Fast 6/8						
Count						

63. Write the number symbols and foot symbols above each note/rest for the following rhythmic sequences. Write the counting syllables below each note/rest.

______________________________ (Name)

64. Complete the notation for the following GAMES.

	r/6/3	2/6	3	r/2	6	r/4
Foot						
? 4						
Count						
? 2						

65. Write the number symbols and foot symbols above each note/rest for the following rhythmic sequences. Write the counting syllables below each note/rest. Add bar lines where needed.

66. The notes that represent (5) & (7) look like the notes in a ◯ .

67. In Fast 12/8 time, how many beats are in a measure ? ________

68. The notes that represent (9) (10) (11) (12) (13) (14) (15) look like the notes in a ◯ .

69. Complete the notation for the following GAME.

	9	8	R	4/8	w·d/w·d	4·8/4·8
Foot						
? 4						
Count						

70. Write the number symbols and foot symbols above each note/rest for the following rhythmic sequence. Write the counting syllables below each note/rest. Add bar lines where needed.

Test Answers

1. Optical Illusion
2. Knowledge, Coordination, Concentration
3. Moves evenly, never inbetween; ∨ = 1 beat; \ = 1/2 beat
4. 1 beat divided into equal notes
5. 1 beat divided into 4 equal notes
6. 1 beat divided into 2 equal notes
7. 1 beat consisting of 1 long note
9. THE GAMES OF MUSIC
10. The GAME; the note in disguise; the note in disguise always replaces the (1)'s
11. The bottom number of the time signature
12. The 2 notes that equal the main note/note value chart
13. The 4 notes that equal the main note/note value chart
17. Rhythms that last longer than 1 beat
18. Note in disguise
19. A note without a stem or flag ; 1/2 the size of the note it follows; tied to the note it follows
23. Silent sound
28. C,D,E,F,G,A,B,C
29. 5 lines and 4 spaces
30. G clef, F clef, C clef
32. Bar line; double bar line; measure
33. How many beats per measure
40. Rhythms formed by combining 2 or more different subdivisions within 1 beat
43. Rhythms formed by dividing subdivisions or combinations with the (1)
47. Subdivision; Tie; Combination; Syncopation
48. (4)
52. (2)
55. (3)
56. Dotted quarter note
61. (4)
66. (4)
67. 4
68. (8)

Note Value Chart A

	Foot	¢ 2	Count	8	C 4
(1)					
(2)					
(3)					
(4)					
(6)					
2					
2·					
4					
(R)					

Note Value Chart B

	Foot	¢ 2	Count	8	C 4
R 2					
R 4					
(2/4)					
(4/2)					
(w·/d)					
(w/ē/d)					
(w/e·)					
(r/2)					
(2/r)					

Note Value Chart C

	4/r	r/4	1·/2	1·/4	2/1·	4/1·	r/1·	2/1/2	4/1/4
Foot									
?/2 ¢									
Count									
?/8									
?/4 C									

Note Value Chart D

	2/1/4	4/1/2	1/1/1	4·8/4·8	3/33	2/6	3/6/3	6/3/6	3/r/6
Foot									
?/2 ¢									
Count									
?/8									
?/4 C									

Chart E

	Foot	Fast	Count
1			
3			
6			
2			
R			
3/3/r			
3/r/3			
r/3/3			
r/r/3			

Chart F

	Foot	Fast	Count
3/r/r			
3/3/6			
6/3/3			
3/6/3			
3·/6/3			
3·/6			
6/3·			
3/r/6			
6/3/r			

Chart G

	Foot	Fast	Count
r/6/3			
3/6/6			
6/6/3			
6/3/6			
r/6/6			
6/r/6			
2			
4			
r/r/6			

THE GAMES OF MUSIC REVIEW

EVERY RHYTHM EVER WRITTEN CAN BE PLACED IN 1 OF 4 CATEGORIES !

- *SUBDIVISION*
- *COMBINATION*
- *TIE*
- *SYNCOPATION*

SUBDIVISIONS & COMBINATIONS

Rhythms from each of these 2 categories must be performed in **1 BEAT !**

TIES & SYNCOPATIONS

Rhythms from each of these 2 categories require **more than 1 BEAT !**

SUBDIVISIONS : **1 beat** divided into **equal** notes. The (1) is the time signature note/main note. All other *Subdivisions* are equal divisions of the time signature note. (2) (3) (4).

COMBINATIONS: **1 beat** combining **2** or more **different** *Subdivisions* within **1 beat.** Take the **down beat** from one *Subdivision* and combine it with the **up beat** from a different *Subdivision.* 2/4 4/2 33/3 *The "parents" of the "W" sisters are the (4)'s.*

TIES: Rhythms that last **longer than 1 beat.** To the time signature note, tie more time signature notes, *Subdivisions*, or *Combinations.* (1) (1) = 2 1'/2

SYNCOPATIONS: Rhythms that are formed by **dividing** *Subdivisions* or *Combinations* with the **time signature note.** 2/1/2 2/1/4

3 QUALITIES OF A SUCCESSFUL COUNTER

- *KNOWLEDGE*
- *COORDINATION*
- *CONCENTRATION*

Rhythm Reference Chart

Subdivisions

? 4 Rhythms	Number Symbols	Foot Notes	Counting Syllables	Pronunciation
	(1) (R)		1 / 1 * (1 / 1)	* " wu , un "
	(2) (2/r)		1 , & 1 , (&)	" one , and "
	(3) (3/r/3)		D M U D (M) U	" down-mid-up "
	(4)		1 e , & d	" one-e , an-da"
	(5)		1 2 3 4 5	" one-two-three-four-five "
	(6)		1 2 3 , 4 5 6	" 1-2-3 , 4-5-6 "
	(7)		1 2 3 4 5 6 7	" 1-2-3-4-5-6-sev "
	(8)		1 2 3 4 , 1 2 3 4	" 1-2-3-4 , 1-2-3-4 "

Ties

Rhythms	Number Symbols	Foot Notes	Counting Syllables	Pronunciation
	2 R 2		1_2 (1_2)	" wu_un two_oo "
	2• 3		1_2_3	" wu_un two_oo three_e "
	4 R 4		1_2_3_4 (1_2_3_4)	" wu_un 2_3_4 "
	1'/2 1'/r		1• & / 1 1• (&) / 1	" wu_un dot and "
	2/1' r/1'		1 &2 / 2 (1) &2 / 2	" one and_two_oo "
	1'/4		1• &d / 1	" wu_un dot an-da "
	4/1'		1e &2 / 2	" one-e and two_oo "

Combinations

Rhythms	Number Symbols	Foot Notes	Counting Syllables	Pronunciation
	2/4 r/4		1 , & d (1) , & d	" one , an-da "
	4/2 4/r		1 e , & 1 e , (&)	" one-e , and "
	w'/d		1_1_1 d	" wu_u_un da "
	w/ē/d		1 e_e d	" one e_e da "
	w/e'		1 e_e_e	" one e_e_e "
	w'd/w'd 4'8/4'8		1'd , &' d	" wu_u_un da, a_a_an da " " one da , an da "
	2/6		1 , 4 5 6	" one , 4 5 6 "
	6/2		1 2 3 , &	" 1 2 3 , and "
	33/3		D_D U	" dow_own up "

* The students are to whisper the letters, words, or numbers that appear within " ( ) ".

B-513TG

Rhythm Reference Chart

Syncopation

?/4 *Rhythms*	*Number Symbols*	*Foot Notes*	*Counting Syllables*	*Pronunciation*
	2/1/2		1 & 2 &	" one , and two , and "
	r/1/2		* (1) & 2 &	* " (one) , and two , and "
	2/1/4		1 & 2 & - d	" one , and two , an-da "
	1/1/1		D D U U M M	" dow own u up mi id "

Fast 6/8 Rhythms

?/8 *Rhythms*	*Number Symbols*	*Foot Notes*	*Counting Syllables*	*Pronunciation*
	1 R		1 1 * (1 1)	* " wu , un "
	2 2/r		1 , & 1 , (&)	" one , and "
	3 3/r/3		D M U D (M) U	" down-mid-up "
	6		1 2 3 , 4 5 6	" 1-2-3 , 4-5-6 "

Ties

	2		1 2 (1 2)	" wu un two oo "
	3		1 2 3	" wu un two oo three e "
	4		1 2 3 4 (1 2 3 4)	" wu un 2 3 4 "

Combinations

	33/3 r/r/3		D D U (D D) U	" dow own up "
	3/33 r/33		D M M (D) M M	" down mi id "
	3/3/6		D M U-U	" down mid up-up "
	3/6/3		D M-L U	" down mid-le up "
	6/3/3		D-D M U	" down-down mid up"
	3'/6/3		D M-L U	" dow own-le up"
	6/3/6		D-D M U-U	" down-down mid up-up"
	3/6/6		D M-L U-U	" down mid-le up-up "
	6/6/3		D-D M-L U	" down-down mid-le up "
	1/1/1		D D U U M M	" dow own u up mi id "

* The students are to whisper letters, words, or numbers that appear within " ( ) ".

B-513TG

Rhythm Reference Chart

Subdivisions

?/4 Rhythms	Number Symbols	Foot Notes	Counting Syllables	Pronunciation
	1 R			
	2 2/r			
	3 3/r/3			
	4			
	5			
	6			
	7			
	8			

Ties

Rhythms	Number Symbols	Foot Notes	Counting Syllables	Pronunciation
	2 R 2			
	2· 3			
	4 R 4			
	1·/2 1·/r			
	2/1· r/1·			
	1·/4			
	4/1·			

Combinations

Rhythms	Number Symbols	Foot Notes	Counting Syllables	Pronunciation
	2/4 r/4			
	4/2 4/r			
	w·/d			
	w/ē/d			
	w/e·			
	w·d/w·d 4·8/4·8			
	2/6			
	6/2			
	33/3			

* The students are to whisper the letters, words, or numbers that appear within " ( ) ".

B-513TG

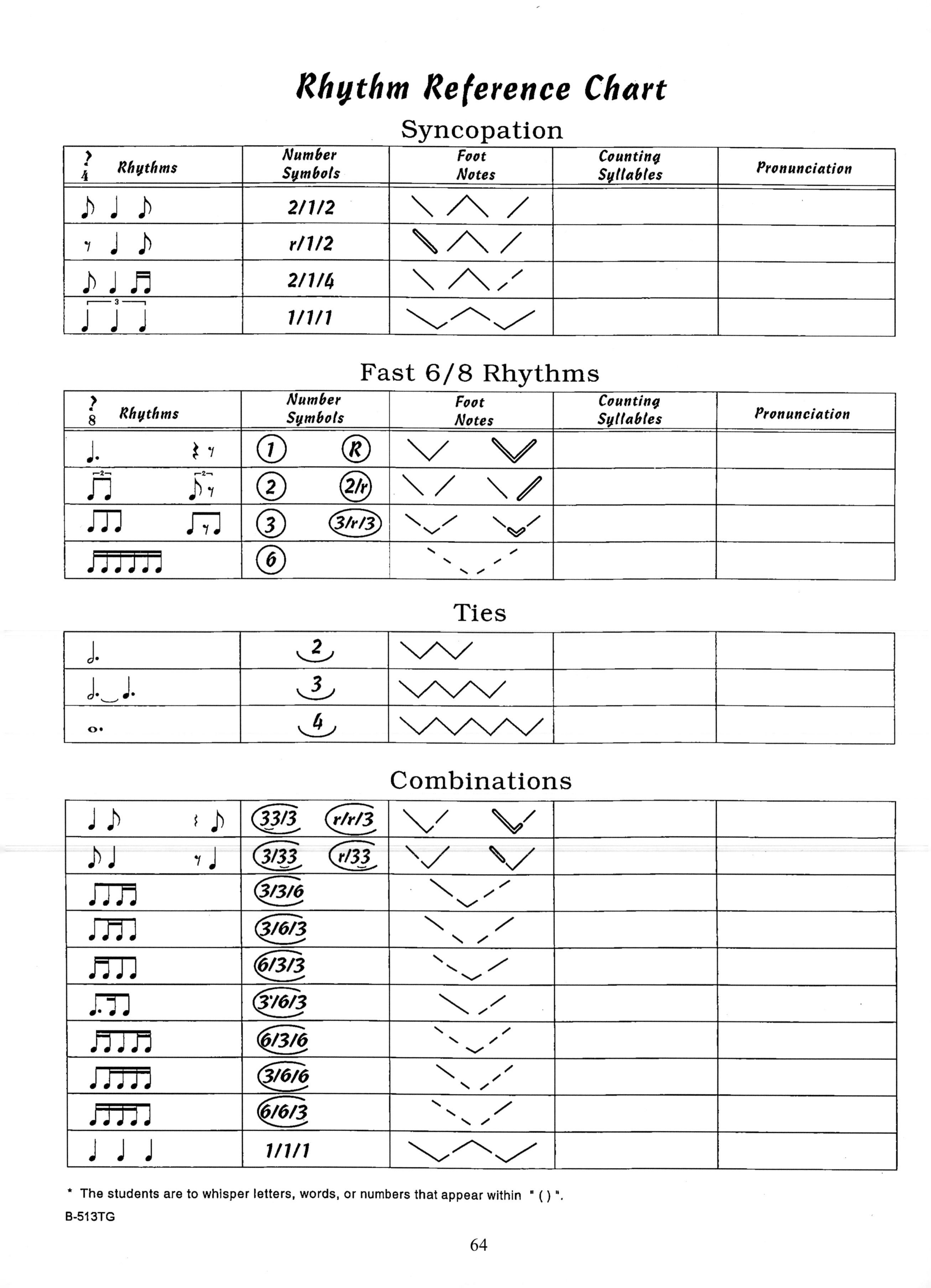

Rhythm Reference Chart

Syncopation

?/4 Rhythms	Number Symbols	Foot Notes	Counting Syllables	Pronunciation
	2/1/2			
	r/1/2			
	2/1/4			
	1/1/1			

Fast 6/8 Rhythms

?/8 Rhythms	Number Symbols	Foot Notes	Counting Syllables	Pronunciation
	(1) (R)			
	(2) (2/r)			
	(3) (3/r/3)			
	(6)			

Ties

	2			
	3			
	4			

Combinations

	33/3 r/r/3			
	3/33 r/33			
	3/3/6			
	3/6/3			
	6/3/3			
	3'/6/3			
	6/3/6			
	3/6/6			
	6/6/3			
	1/1/1			

* The students are to whisper letters, words, or numbers that appear within " ( ) ".

B-513TG

CUMULATIVE CLASS REVIEW

1. "What do musicians call numbers with circles around them?"
   (Place several subdivisions/number symbols on the board)
   SUBDIVISIONS

2. "What do musicians subdivde?"
   BEATS

3. "What is the foot movement for a beat?"
   (Place the down-up V marking above each of the number symbols)
   DOWN-UP

4. Point to each number symbol and ask, "How many equal sounds/notes are in this subdivision?"
   (As the students give you the answer, erase the portion of the V to show 2 or 4 markings, leave the entire V for the subdivision of 1)

5. "What do musicians need to replace the numbers with notes?"
   TIME SIGNATURE

6. "How many numbers are in a time signature?"
   TWO

7. "Which number is important, top or bottom?"
   BOTTOM

8. "What are the possible bottom numbers of a time signature?"
   (Draw a ? on the board to represent the top number. As students give you the bottom numbers, place them under the ?)
   1,2,4,8,16

9. "Are they really numbers?"
   NO

10. "They are?"
    (Draw the note as you point to each number)
    NOTES IN DISGUISE

11. "The note in disguise always replaces the...?"
    (Select a time signature/game and replace all the 1's with the note in disguise)
    1's/ or **SUBDIVISIONS OF 1's**

12. "How do musicians find the answers for the 2's and 4's?"
(Remind the students that they locate the **note in disguise** in the Note Value Chart and then refer to the 2 and 4 notes above)

NOTE VALUE CHART

13. "For every note there is an equal ...?"
(Draw each note on the board and then the corresponding rest)

REST

14. "Rests are silent ....?"

SOUND

15. "What do musicians tie together for Tie Rhythms?
(Illustrate on board)

THE NOTE IN DISGUISE

16. "What does a dot do to a note?"
(Illustrate on board)

ADDS ½ THE LENGTH OF THE NOTE IT FOLLOWS

17. "What do musicians combine to make Combination Rhythms?"
(Illustrate on board)

DIFFERENT SUBDIVISIONS

18. "What do musicians use to syncopate rhythms?"
(Illustrate on board)

THE NOTE IN DISGUISE

19. " What is the **note in disguise** for fast 6/8 ?"

THE DOTTED QUARTER NOTE

20. "What is the most important subdivision for fast 6/8 ?"
(Tie the 3 eight notes together to illustrate why the dotted quarter note is the note in disguise. Illustrate other fast 6/8 rhythms by tying or dividing eighth notes)

SUBDIVISION OF 3

Glossary

Beat .... A specific length of time, establishing the boundaries for all rhythms.

Combinations .... Rhythms that combine 2 or more different subdivisions within 1 beat.

Counting .... The process used to control the length of sound and silence.

Games of Music .... The bottom number of a time signature/note in disguise. The note or rest that is to receive 1 beat.

Notes .... Musical symbols used to represent the pitch and length of sound.

Note/Rest Values .... Equal divisions of notes or rests.

Number/Letter Symbols .... Numbers and letters used to link rhythmic feel with rhythmic recognition.

Pulse .... The rhythmic sensation due to the performance of more than 1 beat of sound.

Rests .... Musical symbols used to represent "silent" sound.

Rhythm .... The performing of various lengths of sound or sound and silence.

Sight Reading .... The ability to quickly transfer musical notation to ones performance medium on the first attempt.

Sizzle .... Sound produced by the teeth, tongue and air. Used to associate rhythmic feel to rhythmic recognition.

Subdivision .... Rhythms that divide 1 beat into equal notes/rests.

Syncopation .... Rhythms formed by dividing subdivisions or combinations with the subdivision of 1.

Ties .... Rhythms that require more than 1 beat to perform.

Time Signature .... The fraction sign at the beginning of a song. The bottom number represents the "note in disguise" that replaces the subdivision of 1's, and whose top number indicates how many beats per measure.